1,001 Ways to Save the Earth

1,001 Ways to Save the Earth

Joanna Yarrow

CHRONICLE BOOKS
SAN FRANCISCO

First published in the United States in 2007
by Chronicle Books LLC.

Library of Congress Cataloging-in-Publication Data available.

ISBN-10: 0-8118-5986-X
ISBN-13: 978-0-8118-5986-8

Manufactured in Singapore

Conceived, created, and designed by Duncan Baird Publishers.

Editor: James Hodgson
Managing Designer: Suzanne Tuhrim
Managing Editor: Christopher Westhorp
Commissioned artwork and cover illustration: Andrew Selby
Cover design: Adam Machacek

Typeset in AT Shannon

Distributed in Canada by Raincoast Books
9050 Shaughnessy Street
Vancouver, British Columbia V6P 6E5

10 9 8 7 6 5 4 3 2

Chronicle Books LLC
680 Second Street
San Francisco, California 94107

www.chroniclebooks.com

Publisher's Note: This book is printed using mineral oil-free vegetable-based inks on paper produced from pulp obtained from sustainably managed forests, and from paper mills that meet environmental standard ISO 14001.
It is 100 percent recyclable.

How can I help to protect the rainforest—the lungs of the planet?

What arguments should I use to persuade my friends to recycle waste?

What can one citizen do to help protect the ozone layer?

1,001 WAYS TO SAVE THE EARTH

Is nuclear power a threat to our world or the answer to its problems?

How can I conserve energy around the home—and save money at the same time?

How can I help to ensure the best possible legacy for my grandchildren—a habitable world?

Would it really make a difference if I walked more, or caught the bus or train, and drove less?

Do my shopping and eating habits affect the health of the planet?

INTRODUCTION

Unless you've spent the last few years living on a desert island or a mountaintop, you'll probably have noticed that our planet seems to be in trouble. But however much you care, it can be hard to know how to help when you're already leading a busy life. This book is designed to inspire and guide anyone who wants to play an active part in caring for the environment, but who's at a loss about where to start.

The state of the environment was once a fringe discussion. A well-publicized campaign to save a cuddly jungle animal or pretty piece of land in our neighborhood might have caught our attention occasionally, but it was easy to dismiss eco-warriors and -worriers as well-meaning "alternative" types, whose concerns over the fate of a few obscure beetles and far-flung swamps had no bearing on the lives of anyone else. Nature seemed so resilient, the globe so large, and scientists so clever that it was hard to imagine our lifestyles could really dent its web of life in any significant way.

But times have changed fast, and the frighteningly perilous state of the Earth is now mainstream news. Evidence from around the world shows that a small number of the Earth's inhabitants (we humans) are causing irreversible damage to the planet, pushing its support systems out of kilter, and jeopardizing the future of all the other species we share it with.

Our destructive impact is evident in every part of the globe. For example, fish are changing sex as a result of exposure to manmade toxins, and species are becoming extinct at the fastest rate in history as their habitats are destroyed. Climate change associated with the burning of fossil fuels brings its own tales of woe—from the drowning or starving of polar bears as the ice they hunt on melts earlier each year, to the threat posed to the homes of hundreds of millions of people by rising sea levels.

These are no longer problems that our grandchildren might have to deal with if they're unlucky. They're happening now and happening fast. Many scientists predict that unless we significantly reduce our impact on the environment, within the next couple of decades, we'll pass a point where runaway climate change is unleashed—a point beyond which the planet will change irreversibly, whatever we do.

Fundamentally, the planet itself will be fine. It has weathered many changes, and—perhaps short of complete nuclear holocaust—it will weather whatever we throw at it. But it won't necessarily survive the onslaught we're currently subjecting it to in a condition that's comfortable—or even endurable—for the human species.

These problems can seem very distant from the reality of our everyday lives. When you've got to get the kids off to school, pay the mortgage, fit in a hair appointment, get the gardening done, write a work report, and visit the in-laws, saving the planet can seem like one chore too many.

But you don't necessarily need extra time or money, or the powers of a superhero, to do your part to look after the planet. The damage we're wreaking is a direct result of the way we choose to live our lives. Pretty much everything we do has an impact on the natural world. So changes to any of our daily activities, from the moment we get up in the morning until we go to bed at night (hopefully between organic cotton sheets), represent an opportunity to look after the planet better without adding too much to our "to do" list. Anything, from the food we eat and the way we store and cook it to the way we get to work and the work we do, our shopping habits, the clothes we wear and the way we launder them, the way we bathe, play sports, and entertain ourselves, and how we maintain our home, can be changed in simple but significant ways for the benefit of the planet.

You don't need to be a paragon of virtue to make a difference. There's something in planet care for even the most selfish of us. And there are side benefits, including saving money, losing weight, getting fitter, keeping your kids amused, outdoing your neighbors, or simply fostering a warm inner glow.

Prioritizing the planet is a mindset you can apply to everything you do, from planning a party to planning your retirement, getting away from it all to getting a loan. Excitingly, as the challenges of living sustainably become more apparent, people and organizations around the world are responding with a range of creative actions, innovations, and initiatives, from the tiny to the colossal.

This book contains an eclectic mix of ways you could help to protect and enhance the planet and develop a more just and equitable society for everyone living on it. Some are tiny modifications in personal habits, which, repeated daily, could have a huge impact over a lifetime. Others are inspiring ideas for longer-term lifestyle choices, which require bigger commitment or investment. You will also find discussions of key environmental issues, such as climate change, GMO foods, and renewable energy sources. There's no single recipe for a perfectly planet-friendly life, but there are definitely more than 1,001 positive actions you can add to the mix . . .

Whether you dip into it for occasional inspiration or read it from cover to cover, I hope that this book will stop you from feeling that there's nothing you can do to help look after this wonderful planet. Find the suggestions you like, incorporate them into a personalized program of lifestyle changes, and let's live on the Earth as if we intended to stay!

Joanna Yarrow, Beyond Green (www.beyondgreen.co.uk)

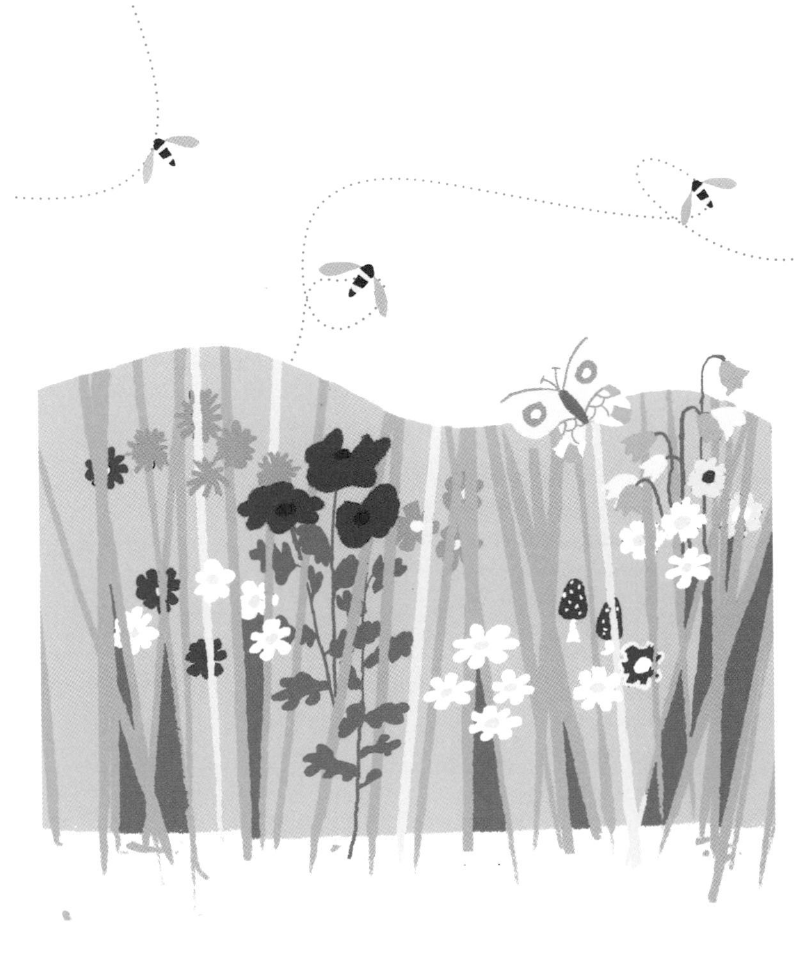

1 **Offset your flight's CO_2** Aviation may soon account for 15 percent of all greenhouse gas emissions. When there's no alternative to flying, why not help mitigate the environmental costs? Specialist companies (see page 373) allow you to calculate online your seat's proportion of the flight's emissions and negate it by buying "offsets"—a contribution they invest in CO_2 (carbon dioxide) reduction measures, such as planting trees. On a return flight between New York and London your 1½ tons of CO_2 incurs a $15 offset.

---

2 **SPEAK UP** If you see something you think might be pollution—from trash dumped in a park to foamy scum on the surface of a river—notify your local government or environmental agency. Perhaps someone else has already pointed it out, but it's far better for the problem to be reported twice than not at all.

---

3 **Lusher lawns** Longer grass retains moisture better than short turf, so in hot weather let your lawn grow to at least 1½ in. before you cut it to avoid brown patches and unnecessary watering.

4 BUY SOFTWOOD Does your furniture need to be made out of a rare, slow-growing hardwood when you could use attractive, fast-growing (and so more readily renewable) spruce, cedar, or pine?

---

5 Extremely cool Keep a pitcher or bottle of tap water in the fridge. This will mean that you don't waste water waiting for it to come cold out of the faucet.

6 Donate your weekend shave Save on water, foam, and balm by forgoing your daily shaving ritual at the weekend. Your partner might object to your stubble, but just remind them, it's all for the greater good . . .

7 Don't be floored by choices Instead of artificial fibers, choose a natural floor covering such as sisal, jute, coir, or cork.

8 Keep pet birds exotic Colorful parrots, macaws, and other birds are better off left in their natural environment, instead of being dragooned as domestic pets. Undermine trapping and trafficking by not buying. Instead, save for a trip to the rain forest—setting aside enough to offset your flight's CO_2 emissions (see page 12), of course. There you can see birds flying in their natural habitat, and your money will help to support local communities trying to keep things that way.

9 **Wonderful baking soda** Forget fancy cleaning products: they're expensive and we need contact with some of the germs they obliterate to keep up our natural defenses. Use cheap and effective baking soda as an all-purpose cleaner, scouring powder, polish, and fungicide. And with what's left, do some baking.

10 **Wake up and smell the coffee** Shun chemical-containing "air fresheners," and make use of naturally satisfying aromas, such as potpourri—or fresh bread and coffee!

11 **Read all about it** Newspaper is one of the easiest materials to recycle. Every time you recycle a pile of papers a yard high, you save a tree from the chop.

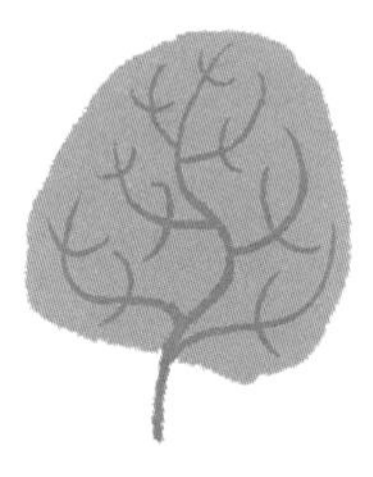

12 **Be a beekeeper** The humble bee is a real friend to humankind, not only because it generates honey and wax but also because it pollinates wildflowers, garden plants, and crops that would otherwise become extinct. Indeed, it's been estimated that without these buzzy insects the planet would last for only 60 years. By cultivating a small "hobby hive," we can support bees in their vital work—it requires only about half an hour's work per week to produce jars and jars of delicious, home-grown honey.

13 Cut your carbs Carbon dioxide (CO_2) is an essential component of life on Earth. It traps some of the sun's rays in the atmosphere, warming the planet to a habitable temperature. But human activity—particularly the burning of fossil fuels—is raising the amount of CO_2 in the atmosphere to a level higher than at any time in the last 650,000 years. It's acting like a blanket that's too thick, warming the Earth to a degree that could fundamentally alter the climatic balance that allows life as we know it to flourish.

All manner of activities—from breathing to driving cars—produce CO_2. The average American generates around 20 tons of CO_2 per year, from all activities. If we're to limit climate change, scientists estimate that we will each need to reduce our so-called "carbon footprint" to less than 2½ tons per year. That may sound draconian, but it's achievable through a series of lifestyle changes.

Visit an online carbon-footprint calculator (see page 370) to **find out how much CO_2 you're producing per year (14)** and follow the suggestions in this book to curb your carbon habit. **Resubmit your details every few months (15)** and watch the pounds drop off your annual emissions.

16 **Water torture** There's no point heating water to near boiling for bathing, as you'll just have to mix it with cold. Save energy by lowering your water-heater thermostat to 140 degrees Fahrenheit.

17 **Worship the sun** Make the most of the sun's warmth by using the sunniest rooms in your house more during winter. If you live in a cold climate, when it's time to repaint the exterior of your house, **choose a dark color to absorb more heat (18)**. Desert-dwellers should choose a pale exterior.

19 **Keep in tune** Have your heating system serviced regularly—both for safety and to ensure that it's performing as efficiently as possible.

When regular servicing's no longer enough and you need to get a new furnace, **invest in a super-efficient condensing-gas model (20)**, which could use up to 30 percent less energy than your existing furnace.

21 **Directional heating** If your heating system uses radiators, make sure you're heating your rooms, rather than your walls, by fitting reflective material such as aluminum foil behind them.

Another approach is to **fit a shelf a couple of inches above a radiator (22)** to guide the heat into the room rather than up the wall.

---

23 **BLESSED RELEASE** Open radiator valves regularly to remove any trapped air and ensure they're working at maximum efficiency.

---

24 **Under wraps** In cold climates, up to half the heat used in the home is lost through exterior walls. If you have cavity walls, you can keep your home snug by having insulating material injected into the cavities through a small hole in each wall. Solid walls can be insulated by adding a layer of rigid insulation material.

Installing attic insulation (25) is a straightforward and cost-effective way to minimize your heating bills and cut your home's CO_2 emissions. To be most effective, the insulating layer should be at least 7 in. thick.

Whether insulating your walls or your loft, try to **use a recycled or environmentally benign insulating material (26)**, made from, for example, recycled newspaper, sheep's wool, blue jeans, or cellulose fibre.

27 Thrive in an urban jungle Modern furniture and electronic equipment can emit enough chemicals to make the air in our homes and offices more hazardous than the air outdoors. Some plants are particularly effective absorbers of these harmful pollutants—clean up the air indoors and brighten your work and living space by surrounding yourself with spider plants, Boston ferns, rubber plants, and palms.

28 **Beyond fossil fuel** By 2030, global energy demand is projected to be two-thirds higher than it is today. Relying solely on fossil fuels isn't an option: reserves are finite; the potential damage to the environment, infinite.

Renewable energy sources, such as wind, wave, and solar power, are an increasingly viable alternative. Apart from being carbon-neutral (emitting negligible CO_2 into the atmosphere), they offer numerous other advantages. For example, they rely on free fuel, so running costs are minimal, avoiding the economic chaos that fuel price fluctuations can cause. They are also far less vulnerable to terrorist attack than conventional energy sources.

Renewable resources currently provide only a small share of global energy production, but wind and solar power are the fastest-growing energy sources in the world. The costs of these and other renewables are falling rapidly as technologies become more advanced, manufacturing is automated, and economies of scale are achieved through increased production volumes.

If progress continues at the current rate, up to a billion people could be served with renewable energy in the next decade, and renewables could account for a third to a half of world energy production by 2050.

29 **Words of encouragement** If you're feeling sad, apathetic, empty, afraid, angry, or guilty about the state of the world, the healing work of the American eco-philosopher, facilitator, and activist Joanna Macy may help inspire you to action. In books such as *Coming Back to Life*, she shares tried and tested practices for reconnecting ourselves to the natural world.

---

30 **LOOKING TO THE FUTURE** Encourage children you know to write vows to look after the planet, and help them to create a "promise tree" with their vows on paper leaves.

---

31 **Stub it out** Tobacco growing involves heavy pesticide and herbicide use. Much of this toxic sludge ends up in the soil and in waterways, causing significant environmental damage in some of the world's poorest countries. The rest ends up in your lungs.

32 **No time to spare** Play an active role in protecting the web of life that supports us all by getting involved in a conservation project. You could go it alone by creating some new habitats in your garden, or join in a bigger project run by a conservation organization (see page 369). Ideally do both—the Millennium Ecosystem Assessment estimates that 10–30 percent of species are under serious threat, so we need to get moving.

33 **Don't get palmed off** Palm oil is found in many products, from face creams to margarine. While it may impart a smooth texture, its production gives ecosystems a rough ride. Palm plantations are replacing huge swathes of ecologically valuable Indonesian forests and their inhabitants (including the last few orangutans and Sumatran tigers). So look for products containing less destructive plant oils, such as canola, sunflower, or olive.

34 **Crumb-free keyboard** When you're at work and need to go out to buy lunch, relax and eat your food in a café, instead of taking it back to your desk—you won't need to use any packaging, and you'll be more relaxed when you get back to the office.

35 **Be a smart cook** Cooking meals from scratch is a healthier, more energy-efficient option than buying processed food or takeouts, but you can save even more energy by not being a slave to the cookbook. For example, if you **turn the oven off ten minutes before the time stated in the recipe (36)**, the residual heat will keep the food cooking. Similarly, **don't bother preheating the oven (37)** unless you're cooking pastries, bread, or a soufflé.

38 **Less speed, more fuel** Attention all speed freaks! Driving at 50mph is 25 percent more fuel-efficient than driving at 70mph. And you're much less likely to wrap your car around a tree.

39 **Say what you need** Whether it be your city council or the manager of your local convenience store, people will be more likely to offer you the service you want if they know what you're looking for. So be sure to ask manufacturers and retailers to provide goods and services that help you in your mission to go green.

40 **Naturally lighter** Help your home to work in harmony with sunshine. By painting interior walls in pale colors and keeping your windows clean, you'll make your rooms look brighter and reduce the need for artificial light.

41 **VIRTUOUS CYCLE** Teach a child to ride a bicycle and set them up with a healthy, eco-friendly, economical habit for life. Every four-mile trip by bike rather than car prevents around 15 pounds of air pollution and builds a strong heart—frequent cyclists are as fit as people ten years younger who don't do regular exercise.

42 **Under pressure** Rev up the cooking process by using a pressure cooker, which will cut cooking times and should use 50–75 percent less energy than a normal saucepan.

43 **Keep it sealed** Covering food (or ice cubes) in your fridge or freezer (ideally with a lid or plate rather than foil or plastic wrap) not only stops the food from drying out but prevents the moisture it contains from condensing as ice on the walls of the appliance. A fridge or freezer with iced-up walls uses more energy and needs defrosting more often.

44 **Cold facts** Fridges and freezers are probably the most expensive electrical items to run in our homes, so make sure they're not using more energy than they need to. Next time you have to buy a new one, **choose the most energy-efficient model (45)** you can find. You'll recoup your investment in saved energy during the first few years of the machine's life.

Whatever the age of your appliance, don't make it work harder than it needs to. **Regulate the internal temperature (46)**: fridges don't need to be colder than 37–41 degrees Fahrenheit and freezers should operate at minus 5 degrees.

Invest in fridge and freezer thermometers if your appliances don't have them built in. To improve efficiency **clean off the coils (47)** at the back of your fridge or freezer and **defrost regularly (48)**—when the ice is ⅛–¼ in. thick. **Position your fridge and freezer in a cool spot (49)**, well away from the stove and with a gap behind of at least 2½ in. for air to circulate. **Check that the door seal is tight (50)** by putting a piece of paper in the door: if the paper slips out when the door's closed, you may need to change the seal to prevent cold air from escaping. **Wait for cooked food to cool (51)** before you put it in the fridge, and **don't leave the door open for longer than necessary (52)**—it's only your groceries that need refrigerating, not your kitchen.

53 **Star performance** If you're worried that your current fridge is wasting energy, visit the Energy Star website (see page 371). There you will find a handy calculator to help you work out how much money you could shave off your energy bill by switching to an Energy Star-accredited model. The older your fridge, the less efficient it's likely to be. If you do decide to replace your fridge, make sure you dispose of the old one responsibly (see page 136).

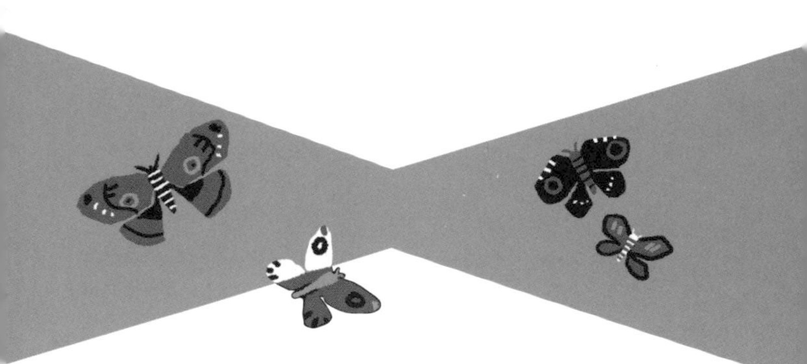

54 Put mothballs into mothballs The distinctive smell of mothballs comes from the evaporation of their toxic chemical ingredients, naphthalene and dichlorobenzene, which are both bio-accumulative. Instead of noxious-smelling balls, why not use a natural moth-repellant? Add to your closet and drawers cedar disks, lavender bags, or a mix of herbs and spices such as rosemary, cinnamon, cardamom, and cloves to keep moths at bay the sweet-smelling way.

55 A more seductive candlelight Traditional paraffin-wax candles are petroleum-based. Once lit, they emit toxins such as acetone, benzene, lead, and mercury into the air. Beeswax and soy candles, by contrast, are toxin free. Not only do they provide a healthier atmosphere for romantic dinners for two, but the pleasant experience will last longer, as these natural candles burn for 50 percent longer than synthetic ones.

56 **Plastic not so fantastic** When buying presents for children, steer clear of toys made from PVC, which can leach noxious chemicals when the surface is scratched, and emits carcinogenic toxins if burned. Toys that don't contain this harmful form of plastic are labeled "PVC-free." Better still, try to **find toys made from materials such as wood or fabric (57)**, which can be just as appealing to kids. Try also to **avoid toys that need batteries (58)**, which are energy intensive and can leak toxins when trashed. Get yourself a set of rechargeable batteries and a charger (ideally solar) to run any electric items your children can't do without.

59 **Think bigger** Try adapting some of the changes you're making in your personal life to other contexts. Let people at your school, workplace, place of worship, or favorite store know what you're up to. They may want to get involved, which will help you to make a much greater impact.

60 **Eat slowly** Take time to enjoy the whole process of preparing and eating food in ways that have developed over centuries. Become part of the international Slow Food movement, which aims to "promote gastronomic culture, develop a taste education, conserve agricultural biodiversity, and protect traditional foods at risk of extinction."

61 **Less is more** It requires much more land, water, and energy to derive food from animals than from vegetables. For example, in the U.S. it takes 70 quarts of water to produce a pound of wheat (one sixtieth of a bushel), but a whopping 2,100 quarts to produce a pound of beef. If life without hamburgers sounds just too bleak, try cutting down your meat consumption to one or two meals each week, and use the money you've saved to splurge on locally produced, organic meat specialties.

62 **Glug down some organic milk** If you're trying to "go organic," milk is a good place to start. The price difference is marginal, but the health benefits are significant: organic milk contains much higher levels of nutrients—for example, up to two-thirds more omega 3 essential fatty acids—than intensively farmed milk.

63 **My darling turpentine** Next time you've got paintbrushes to clean, use real turpentine instead of turps substitute or white spirit. It's distilled from pine and so smells delicious. And, most importantly for the health of those around you, it's low in volatile organic compounds (see page 186).

64 **Genuine article** Choose real corks rather than plastic ones. Not only are they easier to get out of the bottle, but they're made from a renewable resource, grown in forests that support a huge variety of wildlife, including endangered species, such as the Iberian lynx. And when you've finished with them you can collect them to use as fire lighters or put them on your compost pile.

65 **Little by little** If you try to take on too many of the suggestions in this book at once, you may end up doing most of them only a few times before lapsing. To avoid eco-evangelist burnout, try to add a few of your favorite suggestions to your routine each week and build up your portfolio of lifestyle changes gradually.

66 Commune with peers If you've got a good energy-saving tip you'd like to share, if you need something, or if you've got something to offer, put a notice up in the local stores.

---

67 THINK AROUND THE BOX A bored child can be brought to life by a simple cardboard box, which a fertile imagination can turn into anything from a den to a spaceship. Before you recycle the box, let your child have hours or even days of fun with it.

68 **Know your plastics** Plastic comes in many different forms, and each type must be recycled separately. The only way of sorting plastics is by hand, so play your part by acquainting yourself with the identifying code numbers for different types of plastic, which are usually embossed within a mobius loop symbol, choosing the types that are most easily recyclable, such as PETE (code number 1) and HDPE (code number 2), and putting them into the appropriate recycling system when you've finished with them.

69 **Changing times** Your baby's likely to plow through around 5,000 diapers before he or she is toilet trained. If you use disposables, that's about a ton of diapers to landfill. So try reusable diapers—modern ones are surprisingly streamlined and easy to handle. Using reusables will save you a huge amount of cash. So if you find the laundering process an unpleasant chore, why not spend some of the money you've saved on **subscribing to a local diaper service (70)**? They'll provide a constant supply of clean cloth diapers and collect the used ones from your home. Their large-scale laundry process is also more efficient than washing at home.

However, when you're away from home, reusable diapers may not be practical. For road trips, **use disposable diapers made from recycled materials (71)**. Check that they don't contain latex, perfumes, gels, or dyes. Such synthetic ingredients can be toxic when absorbed into babies' delicate skin, and cause pollution when buried or incinerated. Certain brands are fully biodegradable, so you can put them on a compost pile!

72 **Don't wipe out your savings** The diaper isn't the only area of baby care to have been invaded by throwaway products. Disposable baby wipes are also rife, but you can easily do without them by using washable wipes—either bought or homemade from old material. You'll save a pile of money and a mountain of waste, and protect your child and the environment from the synthetic chemicals found in many disposable wipes.

73 **Children's menu** Make your own baby food using locally grown or home-grown organic fruit and vegetables. A batch of pureed fruit and veggies frozen in small containers will last for ages. It will be fresher, cheaper, tastier, and more nutritious than store-bought versions, and quick and easy to make.

74 **Winged victory** Butterflies and moths are becoming ever rarer as their habitats are destroyed by agriculture and other human activity. Do your bit to redress the balance by planting butterfly-friendly flowering plants such as lilac, buddleia, honeysuckle, and evening primrose, and enjoy the color that the flowers and butterflies bring to your garden.

75 **Breast is best** Not all mothers are able to breast-feed, but if it's an option, breast milk is not only more healthful for your baby, but much healthier for the environment. It comes without any packaging, and doesn't require fossil fuel energy to make it!

If breast-feeding isn't possible, **choose organic baby formula (76)**. That way, you won't be feeding your baby the traces of antibiotics, pesticides, and fertilizer often found in nonorganic versions.

77 **Choose a shortlived casket** Your coffin is one thing that doesn't need to be built to last! Cardboard or wicker coffins decompose quickly into the soil. Ask for one in your will, and make your loved ones aware of your wishes.

78 **Common enemy** If we are to solve problems such as global warming, we will have to put national interests to one side. The more that people from different nations understand each other, the easier this will be. One way to play your part would be to join SERVAS (www.servas.org), an international peace organization that fosters networks of hosts and travelers, encouraging personal contacts between people from different parts of the world.

---

79 **A PLACE OF YOUR OWN** Find a "magic spot" in a patch of nature (however small), and go there whenever you need space to reflect.

---

80 **Buzz off** Keep flies away naturally with essential oils such as citronella, mint, eucalyptus, and clove.

81 **Thoughts at the checkout** Ask yourself whether the item you're about to buy is something you really need. Will it make you more fulfilled? If not, try doing something else to nurture yourself instead, like eating good food, doing something special with a friend, going for a walk, or planning something you've been interested in for ages.

82 **Cut down your wine miles** As you'll know if you've ever lugged a case back from the liquor store, bottles of wine take some carrying. So, minimize your contribution to the environmental headache of hauling this heavy treat around the globe by favoring wines produced as close to home as possible.

83 **Dressed for warmth** If your water heater tank is a bit past its prime, wrap it up in a fiberglass blanket. One of these can be picked up cheaply at a home center, and within a few months it will have paid for itself in lower heating bills.

84 **Piping hot** Make sure water inside pipes stays hot—particularly during long trips through cold areas such as the garage—by wrapping any exposed pipework in insulating material.

85 **Decondition yourself** Minimize your dependence on energy-hungry air conditioning by tackling heat the natural way. **Shade sunny windows (86)** with draperies and shades or blinds inside, and trees and climbing plants outside. **Open windows at night (87)** to allow cross-ventilation, but keep them shut during the day.

Install a large ventilating fan in the attic (88), and run it in the evening with windows and attic hatch open to pull cooler air into the house, which will drive hot air into the roof space.

If you must use air conditioning, go for a low energy-rated system (89), and make sure all the ducts are properly sealed. And use it only when it's really necessary!

90 Window-wise Much of a building's heat can be lost through its windows. You can minimize this waste by installing storm windows or double-pane windows, ideally using low-emissivity glass, which further limits heat loss. If that's too big a project, **fix plastic insulating film (91)** over each pane for a similar (although less perfectly transparent) effect at a fraction of the price.

92 Curtain magic Not only do draperies create a cozy atmosphere, but they can be as effective at keeping warmth in as an extra layer of glazing. To keep rooms warm during winter, **close draperies (or shades, blinds, or shutters) at dusk (93)**, and open them in the morning to let the sun's heat in during the day. And to keep rooms cool during summer, leave curtains and blinds closed during the day and open them in the evening.

94 **Bus stop** The good old school bus hasn't got a completely clean slate when it comes to environmental issues. When they stop to pick up and deliver children, bus drivers normally leave their engines running, and this idling causes a lot of pollution, especially in urban areas. Excessive idling can also damage the engine. Many school districts have "idling reduction programs"; if yours does not, see if you can get one started.

95 **Little helpers** Put your children in charge of some green tasks around the home—such as checking that lights and appliances are switched off, looking after the composting, or feeding the birds—and reward them for doing well. Find something they enjoy, and the habits are likely to last a lifetime.

96 **Dematerialize your child's school** Ask the staff to match your own green efforts by cutting back on energy and waste on their turf. **Getting rid of vending machines (97)** stocked with canned drinks and overpackaged snacks is a good place to start.

98 **Give it like you mean it** Make a friend a present out of something that's significant to you—perhaps a book from your collection that you have read and particularly enjoyed. Or **devote time to make a gift (99)**: bake a cake or frame some photos of a happy time you've spent together.

100 **Eat before you shop** It's frightening how much food the average household throws away. Studies show that we buy more food if we shop when hungry. So a good meal before you hit the stores, combined with a proper shopping list, helps you to buy only what you need, and reduce this wasteful, expensive, and (ultimately) smelly food glut.

101 **Natural deterrents** Slugs and snails are some of the most destructive invaders the average gardener has to deal with. Fortunately, there are numerous harmless alternatives to chemical pellets, which should be avoided as they kill not only the pests but also beneficial creatures, such as frogs. Slugs and snails like damp conditions, so you can **protect vulnerable plants with a mulch of rough material (102)**, such as sand, gravel, or even crunched-up eggshells. These greedy gastropods are also deterred by copper, which gives them a mild electric shock: to steer them away from container plants, **attach a ribbon of copper tape (103)**, at least 2 in. wide, around the pot.

The simplest—and perhaps most effective—way to deprive slugs and snails of a damp dining environment is to **water your plants first thing in the morning (104)**, rather than in the evening when your unwanted guests are at their most active.

105 **Labor and energy saving** Running a dishwasher can actually have less impact on the environment than doing dishes by hand if you choose a water- and energy-efficient model and put it on only when there's a full load, using a low-temperature setting, an air-dry (not heated-dry) option, and eco-friendly dishwasher powder or tablets. Also, **remember that it's not necessary to pre-rinse items (106)** unless they're covered with burned-on or dried-on food. For sustained efficiency **regularly clean the filter (107)** at the bottom of the machine.

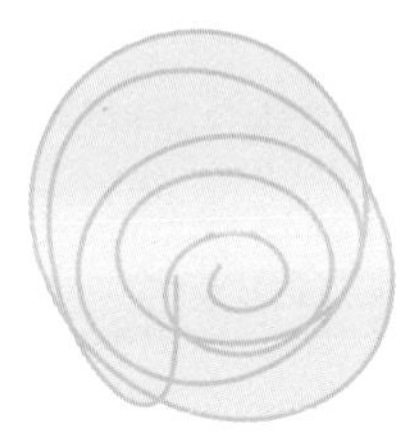

108 **Saline solution** Rather than using a commercial product, use salt to draw out red wine and fruit juice stains.

109 **Distraction tactics** Besides creating a barrier around the plants you don't want slugs and snails to attack (see opposite), you can also tempt them away by setting bait. **Leave uprooted weeds out in a pile (110)** in a damp corner of the garden, instead of putting them straight on the compost pile: slugs and snails like to feed on wilted leaves, which are softer than those on living plants. However, **avoid using beer traps (111)**—small containers of beer buried in the soil. They will attract not only their intended targets to meet a boozy end but also useful creatures, including ground beetles, which actually prey on slugs. And, of course, they're a waste of good beer!

112 **IN TUNE WITH TUNA** High consumer demand means that tuna are being endangered by commercial overfishing. If you're keen to benefit from the fish's health-giving properties, instead of cutting it out entirely, try only buying rod- and line-caught skipjack tuna. These stocks are not threatened by overfishing, and the fishing method avoids killing the huge numbers of other small fish that are caught in commercial nets.

---

113 **Portion control** Pots, watched or otherwise, boil much faster if you put only as much water in them as you need. Boiling one cup of water rather than a full kettle saves enough electricity to power an energy-saving lightbulb for nine hours. If you find it hard to judge the water level, **use a cup or mug to fill the kettle (114)** with the required number of "portions" of water.

115 **Hot pot** Once food's cooked, there's no need to leave the stove on to keep it warm. A few dish towels on the pan's lid will keep the food inside piping hot for quite a while.

116 **Clean your kettle** Keeping your teakettle free from lime deposits makes it more efficient, producing quicker, lower-energy cups of tea and coffee—and they'll taste better, too. Try boiling two cups of distilled white vinegar diluted in a little water to dislodge calcium deposits. Remember to rinse it out afterward!

117 **Screensaver** Make a point of switching off your computer screen each time you leave your desk, especially for longer periods such as your lunch break. A computer in "screensaver" mode uses almost as much energy as it does when it's being used—and, frankly, even the most profound (or profane) of scrolling messages doesn't add that much to office life.

118 **A slow thaw** Plan ahead so you don't need to use a microwave to defrost frozen food. Ideally, let the food thaw in the fridge overnight—its chilliness will leave less work for the fridge to do.

119 **Human radiators** When you host a party, take advantage of the heat generated by your guests to turn the heating down.

120 **Smart planting** For chemical-free gardening success, work with mother nature rather than trying to defy her. **Choose naturally pest-resistant varieties of plants (121)**, and when deciding where to position them, **take account of the type of soil and amount of sun and moisture that suit them best (122)**. If they're in the right conditions, they'll grow strong and be better able to defend themselves against pests and disease. To give additional protection, you could **try companion planting (123)**. This involves mixing together plants that provide useful nutrients for each other or attract predators to prey on the other's pests—for example, tomatoes with carrots, garlic with roses, or nasturtiums with pumpkins, cucumbers, and squash.

124 **Patio heater? Pah!** If you want to invest in some garden hardware, make sure it doesn't cost the Earth. One of the most short-sighted fads of recent years, the liquid propane patio heater wastes energy and produces copious amounts of pollution. Keep warm with extra layers, and a wood-fired brazier or chiminea if you're still cold.

125 **The lights are on . . .** Turning off the light when you leave a room is a very easy and obvious way of saving energy, but a surprising number of empty rooms and even whole buildings blaze with light at night. One way to stop this is to **fit movement sensors (126)** so that lights are activated only when they're needed—including those in domestic outdoor areas.

127 **Bright idea** Switching to compact fluorescent lightbulbs (CFLs) has never been easier, as shapes and sizes are now available to fit many light fixtures. Each bulb uses only about a quarter the electricity of a normal one and they last up to ten times longer, saving you loads of money and energy (as well as the hassle of replacing dead lightbulbs on a regular basis).

128 **Clear as day** Before switching on electric lights, make sure you're making the most of natural daylight. Move your desk near a window—but try not to get distracted by the view!

129 **No energy to spare** Don't waste energy heating or cooling rooms you rarely use. Minimize airflow to registers in spare rooms and keep doors to unused rooms closed. Just make sure that you heat these rooms enough to prevent frozen pipes and damp.

130 **Bedtime routine** If your house is reasonably insulated, you should be able to turn the heating off half an hour before going to bed without noticing any drop in temperature before you crawl under the covers. You should notice a drop in your energy bill, though—of about 5 percent.

131 **Set yourself back** There's no point in keeping your furniture warm when you're away from home, or asleep. Instead, fit an automatic setback thermostat, which can easily be programmed to change the temperature at given hours of the day or night.

132 **Unplugged** Electronic appliances can consume almost as much energy during the time they're in standby mode as they do during the relatively small proportion of the day when they're actively being used. Unplugging electronic equipment can cut your household electricity bill by up to 10 percent. This is particularly important in the case of pieces of digital equipment, which often use more energy than their analogue equivalents.

133 **Get into hot water** Investigate solar energy systems as a source of completely free hot water and heating for your home. You may qualify for an income tax credit if you install one.

134 **Be a jean genie** Three-quarters of a pound of fertilizers and pesticides are used to produce the average pair of jeans. Don't let this happen on your account: buy a pair made from organic cotton. Alternatively, customize a secondhand pair to suit your style. The only resources needed are keen eyes in a thrift shop!

135 **Timeless style** Ask yourself whether you'll like your home's new look in a year or two. Classic, stylish home decoration needs renewing only when it gets shabby, whereas the latest trends in bedding and accessories will quickly appear dated.

136 **The gift of vision** When your lens prescription needs renewing or you want to change your frame style, ask your optician if they participate in a program of donating eyeglasses to developing countries. Or contact your local branch of the Lions Club, which operates such a program.

137 **Slimmer chiller** If you need to buy a new refrigerator, consider scaling down to a smaller model. Although meat, fish, and dairy products need to be refrigerated, many of the other things we put in the fridge would keep just as well in a naturally cool cabinet or pantry (with an air vent installed in a wall if you live in a temperate climate).

138 CUT YOUR CLOTH Minimize the need for cooling or heating in your workplace by persuading your employer to relax its dress code during very hot or cold weather. Take your lead from the Japanese government, which runs a publicity campaign encouraging business people to wear short sleeves in the summer to cut down on air conditioning in their offices.

---

139 Forward-thinking do-it-yourself Have you thought about how you'll get that bed frame you've just assembled back down the stairs when you next move? Use screws instead of nails or glue, so that ready-to-assemble furniture can be dismantled easily and reused, instead of being chopped up and sent to landfill.

140 Natural immunity Our immune systems can cope with—and actually need—exposure to normal household germs. Waging chemical warfare on these organisms alters our homes' microbial balance, encouraging resilient bacteria that can become super-resistant—even to antibiotics. Harsh chemical disinfectants can also affect our central nervous system and organs, and disrupt hormone function. Instead, try natural disinfectants such as tea tree oil, borax, and citrus oils.

141 **Keep a green journal** In a notebook or diary (made from recycled paper, of course!), record each time you and your family take a planet-saving action. You could also write about your feelings—the highs and the lows—as you make progress, or perhaps encounter obstacles.

Your green journal would be a good place to **monitor your utility bills (142)**. Record the number of units of energy or water your household consumes during each billing period. When you've been going for more than a year, you'll be able to compare like with like: winter with winter, summer with summer. Little by little, your journal will enable you to keep track—practically, emotionally, and financially—of your journey toward a greener life.

143 **Occupational hazards** As if the prospect of falling off a ladder weren't bad enough, decorators have a 40 percent increased risk of lung cancer because of their exposure to the volatile organic compounds (VOCs) and solvents found in many paints. So try to use natural paints made from plant and mineral bases or ones with low VOC ratings to avoid the health and environmental problems associated with emissions from solvent-based paints.

144 **Boys' toys** Do you really need or want a complete selection of power tools? Unless you're the most avid do-it-yourself fan, you'll probably use them only once or twice a year. So why not rent professional-grade ones from a rental store on the rare occasions that you do need them, or **club together with neighbors to buy a communal set (145)**? That way, less energy and fewer resources are used to get your jobs done, and you benefit from better products (and more storage space!).

146 **Clean without chlorine** Many detergents and other cleaning products contain chlorine, which when mixed with other compounds can produce toxic gases. Each chlorine atom can destroy tens of thousands of ozone molecules—bad news, given that chlorine concentrations in the upper atmosphere have quadrupled in the last 25 years. So look for chlorine-free detergents, toilet cleaners, disinfectants, and bleach.

147 **Day to remember** As an alternative to another unneeded or unwanted object, give someone you love a gift that takes up space only in the memory, such as a beauty treatment, concert ticket, or trip to a favorite restaurant.

148 **Automate your outgoings** Paying bills will never be entirely painless, but you can eliminate much of the hassle and environmental impact by registering to receive and settle them online. Not only does this save time and cut down on trips to the mailbox, it also reduces paper waste and pollution associated with mail transportation, and trims your postage costs. You can even schedule automatic bill payments so you'll never miss a payment or pay a late fee again!

149 **REDEPLOY YOUR SPARE PAINT** Making paint is an energy-hungry process that produces more than 10 tons of waste for every ton of paint. So make the most of it: instead of letting leftover paint languish in the basement until it's too dried out to use, ask a local school, health center, or community project whether they'd like a fresh lick of paint. There may even be a community paint collection in your area.

---

150 **Read the small print** Many of the unguents we anoint ourselves with to mask our blemishes are hiding more than a few imperfections of their own. It's worth reading the label and looking into the properties and health and environmental impacts of complicated-sounding ingredients (see page 370). Avoid the worst culprits whenever you can. For example, **steer clear of parabens (151)**, such as methylparaben, ethylparaben and propylparaben, which are used as preservatives in cosmetics and toiletries. These chemicals act as "endocrine disruptors," which means that they can mimic, interfere with, or block hormones in humans and animals, and may be linked to breast cancer.

152 **Waste is a dirty word** As an alternative to plowing in resources to cultivate vanilla plants, Japanese scientists have discovered an ingenious way to extract vanilla essence from cow dung, which just goes to show that there's no such thing as a waste product.

153 **Stargazing** Spend a night camping out under the stars with just a groundsheet as basic ground cover to reconnect with the Earth around you and the universe beyond.

154 **Risk-free lacquer** If you want to keep your fingers and toes well dressed, use a water-based nail polish. Unlike solvent-based slicks, these don't contain formaldehyde or phthalates, which can damage both your health and the environment. Water-based versions come in beautiful colors and dry to the touch in just three minutes.

155 **Magic pan** It takes the same amount of time—and energy—to cook a stir-fry as it does to reheat the typical prepackaged meal, and that's not including the energy used to create the prepackaged meal in the first place. The stir-fry will almost certainly taste much nicer and be better for you.

156 **Bamboo bathrobe** Bizarre though it sounds, tough bamboo fiber makes luxuriously soft towels. Bamboo is three times more absorbent than cotton and boasts antibacterial, antistatic, and antifungal properties. It grows quickly and without any need for pesticides, which makes it a fantastically eco-friendly material. Ask any panda!

157 **Put your feet up** Minimize the need to clean your floors by placing doormats inside and outside external doors and asking people to take their shoes off as they come in. Provide a bench and cloth slippers. Who said that saving the planet was hard work?

158 **Squash your trash** Minimize the impact of the trash you can't avoid producing by squashing it before you chuck it. This way it will take up less space in landfill sites or recycling depots—and pummeling it is a great stress-buster as well!

159 **Keep your thermostat cozy** To avoid overheating your home, make sure that the thermostat connected to your furnace is on an internal wall in one of the main living areas in your home, rather than, say, your chilly utility room.

160 **Tasteful waste** If you enjoy making art, stay away from the art-supply store, and take a look in your trashcan instead. With a little imagination, you can transform anything from food containers to leftover building materials into striking artworks. **Take inspiration from the Soweto Mountain of Hope (Somoho) project (161)** in South Africa, which has turned a growing waste problem into an internationally celebrated community art resource.

---

162 **TAKE A LOOK OVER THE FENCE** One of the biggest causes of wasted energy is duplication of resources. We can help to avoid this by sharing more with our neighbors. This can mean anything from car-pooling or taking round a box of produce if it's been a good year in your vegetable plot to investigating setting up a community wind turbine (see page 371).

---

163 **Egg your plants on** Water that has had eggs boiled in it is enriched with calcium. Pouring it on your garden, once it's cooled, rather than down the sink, will save a little water and feed your plants.

164 **Quick-hit stain removal** Here are just a few ways to remove troublesome stains without resorting to environmentally unfriendly cleaning methods. Rub white chalk into oil stains before washing; remove tea, coffee, chocolate, and blood with one part borax to eight parts water; tackle grass stains with glycerin (available from drugstores); and bleach white clothes by laying them out in the sun.

165 **Buff up your polishing** Avoid commercial furniture polishes, which tend to be made from flammable petroleum distillates (linked with lung and skin cancer) and toxic nitrobenzene. Instead, try natural products based on beeswax or olive oil, or you can even **make your own polish (166)** using three parts olive oil to one part vinegar.

167 **The true meaning of dry cleaning** The solvents used in conventional dry cleaning are toxic to humans (especially the unfortunate dry-cleaning staff) and the environment. The simplest way to avoid contributing to this damage is to choose clothes that don't need dry cleaning. You can also **keep clothes fresh for longer between cleans (168)** by airing and brushing them, if appropriate, after each wearing. Some "dry clean only" garments can actually be washed conventionally: **carefully try washing silks and woolens by hand in cold water (169)**. If you feel nervous about this, it's probably best to start with something other than your most treasured silk scarf or tie until you've seen for yourself that it works. Another alternative is to **seek out "wet cleaning" or "green" dry-cleaning services (170)**, which use liquid carbon dioxide or silicon-based solvents in place of harmful substances.

171 **A cooler wash** Clothes very rarely need to be washed at high temperatures. By washing at 100 degrees (warm setting) instead of 140 (hot setting), your washing machine will use 30 percent less energy, and your clothes will last longer.

172 **Say no to junk mail** Protect your home and office from an avalanche of junk mail by registering with a mail preference service (see page 371). To ward off hand-delivered advertisements and leaflets, **place a "no junk mail" sticker on your mailbox (173)**. You may be able to get one from your local government's waste-management department or you can make your own.

174 **Staple diet** If all of the country's 75 million white-collar workers used one fewer staple each day, they'd make a daily saving of 5,500 lbs. of steel—that's about 900 tons a year. Scale down your staple habit, and use (and reuse) paper clips instead.

175 **Cheers!** Suggest to local liquor stores that they lend real glasses free of charge if you buy drinks from them for a party. This should help the stores to win business and their customers to avoid using disposable cups.

176 **TREE OF LIFE** Mark significant events in your life by planting a tree: it will absorb CO_2 and other forms of pollution, provide a home to hundreds of creatures, help create and retain soil, and perform many other valuable ecological functions. It will also be a thing of beauty, and a lasting legacy of your time on Earth. If you don't have access to land on which to plant a tree, a number of organizations will plant one on your behalf.

---

177 **Drying dilemma** It's hard to calculate whether it's more environmentally damaging to dry your hands with an electric dryer (generally powered from non-renewable resources) or paper towels, which contain wood and other valuable resources and when thrown away invariably end up in a landfill. Save yourself this headache by doing neither: carry a small towel in your handbag or backpack instead.

178 **Deter fleas naturally** To keep biting pests away from your furry friends, try smuggling a clove of finely chopped or crushed garlic into your pets' food twice a week. This makes their blood unappetizing to parasites, and so avoids the need for conventional flea powders, collars, and sprays, which contain toxic organophosphates and pesticides associated with animal, human, and environmental health problems. Reinforce this line of defense by **putting rosemary and lavender in your pets' beds (179)** or neem or citrus oil on their coats.

180 **Declare war on packaging** Supposedly designed to make our lives easier, the multilayered packaging that envelops many mainstream grocery products can often be more of a hindrance than a help—and, of course, the effect on the environment is wholly negative. Fortunately, there are numerous ways in which you can help turn the tide. **Buy nonperishable items in bulk packages (181)** or from bulk bins, bringing your own reusable container. **Look for products sold in refillable containers (182)** and make the effort to reuse them. Write to the manufacturers of your favorite brands to ask them to provide this kind of packaging, if they don't already. Similarly, **point out**

the madness (183): if you see a blatantly overpackaged product (cellophane-wrapped coconuts, anyone?), let retailers know how you feel. It's likely they'll look again at how their wares are perceived—it's not in their commercial interests to lose their customers' good will.

As a last resort, **unwrap excessively packaged purchases in the store (184)** and (politely) ask the staff to deal with the waste. That packaging gets added to the cost of our shopping (supermarket shoppers unwittingly spend a sixth or more of their food budget on packaging), so you've got every right to be annoyed.

185 **Dispose of disposables** Most disposable products add little to our quality of life but a lot to waste mountains. Try to use them only in emergencies, and go for less wasteful alternatives. For example, **cover food with a dish, plate, or lid (186)** instead of aluminum foil or plastic wrap, and **wipe up spillages with dish towels and cloths (187)** instead of paper towels. If you're a fan of barbecues and picnics, **buy some unbreakable utensils and dishes (188)** to use in place of flimsy disposable plastic items.

189 **TWO SIDES TO EVERY STORY** Whether printing a long formal report at work or doodling while you chat on the phone, try to use both sides of the paper. You'll get through half the volume of wood and other resources used to make it, and cut CO_2 emissions by 2½ lbs. for every pound of paper you save. **If your printer has a duplex (double-sided) function, make it a default option (190)**—that way, you have to make an adjustment only on the few occasions when single-sided printing is essential.

---

191 **Robust rust remover** To clean metal affected by rust or calcium deposits, use white vinegar, aided with a wire brush if necessary.

192 **Season's greetings** To cut down on the amount of extra paper being transported around the globe at Christmas, send electronic greetings by e-mail. A number of environmental charities offer e-cards via their websites.

For friends who don't have an e-mail address, **buy paper cards directly from an environmental charity (193)**. The

charity is likely to receive more of the proceeds than if you buy charity cards from a mainstream store, and they'll almost certainly be made from recycled card. **Recycle cards you receive (194)**, either by tearing them up and adding them to your compost pile, or—more creatively—by turning them into gift tags for next Christmas.

195 **Collected works** Most people prefer not to race around endlessly on errands. But in our haste to get chores checked off, we often fall into this trap. Save time, energy, and transport costs by looking for ways to pool all your errands into one or two extended circuits each week or split your errands with a neighbor.

196 **Keep it simple** Shun products packaged in mixed materials, such as plastic and foil, as they're complicated and expensive to recycle. If you do find such an item in your cabinets, **try to dismantle it into its constituent materials (197)** before putting it out for recycling.

198 **Longevity** When you're buying equipment for your home or office, make sure it will last. Check that it can be easily repaired and that the manufacturer will supply spare parts. It's also worth investing a little more in products that have a long guarantee.

199 **Getting antsy about ants?** To drive ants out of your home without resorting to extermination, work out how they're getting in, and block the hole, or make the entrance unattractive from an ant's perspective with a squeeze of lemon juice. They also hate talcum powder, chalk, bone meal, charcoal dust, and cayenne pepper, so try making barriers using any of these to persuade them to go elsewhere.

200 **Look before you leap** To avoid wasting paper on typos and other blunders, have a really good look at your document on screen before you hit the print button. Run spellcheck and look at the print preview to make sure that your work is formatted to your satisfaction.

201 **Build a green house** If you're embarking on any kind of building project, you're much more likely to get the eco-friendly results you want if your architect has green credentials (see page 373). Look for one who's up to date on the latest green materials, techniques, and technologies, and the experience should be a pleasant adventure. If they roll their eyes at the first mention of a low-energy lightbulb, you may have a battle on your hands.

202 **As good as new** Look up details of local furniture recyclers. Your outdated dining set could be refinished into someone else's vintage dream.

203 **Grounded vacations** Traveling by land or sea gives you the chance to really take in your surroundings, to have some adventures along the way, and often to arrive almost as quickly as you would by plane (and better rested). Plan a flight-free vacation (see page 373) and not only will you avoid check-in lines, but your trip won't produce anywhere near as much pollution: trains produce 20 times less emissions per passenger mile than planes, and ships almost 200 times less.

204 **Load up the kids with recycling** Schools are generally keen to receive materials such as magazines, newspapers, boxes, and leftover wallpaper—they'll find good second homes in arts and crafts classes, as table coverings, or even as a liner for the school bunny's hutch!

205 **EVERY LAST SCRAP** Recycle all your paper, not just newspapers and magazines. Every ton of paper reused leaves 17 trees standing, looking beautiful, and working hard to absorb CO_2 on our behalf.

---

206 **Protect your clothes with zest** Dried lemon peel is a natural moth deterrent—simply sprinkle pieces in your drawers, or tie a few pieces in cheesecloth and hang them in your closet.

207 **Don't be a water importer** Water's undoubtedly good for your health, but when it comes in a plastic bottle and has been transported long distances, not so good for that of the planet. In the developed world we're lucky enough to have safe drinking water piped, packaging-free, into our homes for a tiny fraction of the cost of bottled water, yet sales of bottles continue to rise.

Try the following steps to kick the bottled-water habit. **Keep a pitcher of tap water in the refrigerator (208)**—when chilled, it's almost indistinguishable from mineral water.

If you're worried about water quality, **invest in a filtration system for your kitchen faucet (209)**. Good intentions are easily eroded when you're out and about—which is also when you tend to be thirstiest. To avoid having to buy endless plastic bottles of water, **pack a small unbreakable drinking bottle and refill it en route (210)**.

211 **In good odor** Synthetic musks (often called "parfum") crop up in an array of products—from cleaning potions to fine perfumes. They're very persistent compounds that aren't broken down easily, and have been found in places as unlikely as mussels, human body fat, breast milk, and fish. They're potential hormone disrupters, and so best avoided. Instead, **choose perfumes based on natural oils (212)** for yourself. And in your home, **make commercial air fresheners unnecessary (213)** by opening windows, absorbing offending smells with a bowl of baking soda dissolved in water, boiling some cinnamon, choosing products perfumed with citronella or other natural oils, or squirting a blend of water and lavender oil from a spray bottle.

214 **Winds of change** Besides reducing your energy use, make sure that the energy you do need comes from a carbon-neutral source. Switching to one of the growing number of companies supplying energy from renewable sources such as wind, sun, and hydropower usually only involves a phone call, after which your home electricity use won't contribute to CO_2 emissions.

215 **Industrial revolution** Find out more about the ideas of the American industrial designer William McDonough by reading his book *Cradle to Cradle* (2002). McDonough is rethinking industrial processes to eliminate waste at source, with the ultimate aim that all byproducts of manufacturing should be suitable either to feed the soil or to be remade, "upcycled," into something else.

216 **Stock your stock pot** Water used for cooking vegetables makes great stock for soups and sauces. If you're not planning to cook again soon, you can still use those nutrients and avoid wasting that water by pouring it onto plants rather than down the drain.

---

217 **ODD SOCKS, EVEN TEMPERATURE** It's a law of nature that every household contains an extended family of neglected odd socks. Give the biggest ones a second career by stuffing them with old rags, stitching the ends closed, and laying them along the bottom of doors to block out chilly drafts.

---

218 **Car clubber** Do you really need a car all day every day? If you need to use a car only occasionally, you could share the cost, avoid the hassles, and minimize the environmental impact of car ownership by joining a car-share plan or car club (see page 373). For a monthly fee and/or hourly rate, you can call upon a well-maintained car whenever you need it, and then hand it back. No more Sundays polishing hubcaps!

219 **Dental arithmetic** Turning the faucet off while brushing your teeth saves up to 10 quarts of water each time. Assuming two brushings a day, that adds up to more than 500,000 quarts over the average person's lifetime.

220 **Only the finest ingredients** If you really want to know what you're putting onto your clothes and skin and sending down your drain, make your own washing powder using a cup of grated natural soap, a cup of washing soda, and a couple of teaspoons of lavender oil.

221 **Lower your flow** Install low-flow aerating fittings to your shower and faucets. These ingenious devices reduce water flow by up to 50 percent, but because they sprinkle in fine jets or mix air bubbles into the water, you feel like you're getting just as wet.

222 **Sink that pot** If you need to wash just a few dishes, don't do them under a running faucet—fill the sink with just enough water to do the job; you'll use only a fraction of the water you would if you kept the faucet on. Ditto for rinsing. If you haven't got a double sink, use a large plastic bowl for that.

223 **Set a cat curfew** Domestic cats can have a huge impact on local wildlife. For example, it's estimated that there are more than 100 million domesticated and semi-wild cats in the United States, and they kill about 1 billion small animals and millions of birds every year. You can help reduce the slaughter by keeping your cat indoors during the hour after sunrise and the hour before sunset, which is when birds are most active. As an extra measure, **give your cat a collar fitted with a bell or sonic device (224)**. These give prey a chance to escape, cutting kill rates by up to 40 percent. Make sure the collar has a quick-release mechanism to stop your cat from choking if it gets caught on something.

225 **Pedal practice** If you don't feel confident about you or your children cycling on roads, enroll your family in a cycling-proficiency course to build up your skills and road awareness. Your local government may offer free or subsidized classes.

226 **Rail versus road** How many business documents, novels, or love letters can you read (or write) while you're driving? Try taking your next long trip by train rather than car. You can enjoy the scenery without endangering anyone's life and avoid the stress of traffic; and if you do some work en route, you'll arrive at your destination with a greater sense of achievement than if you'd been stuck behind the wheel.

227 **Drought-proof your garden** If you have a dry garden, plant drought-tolerant species, such as agapanthus, echinacea, and sedum, which can survive long periods with little or no water (see page 373).

228 **Water wisely** The best times to water the garden are the early morning and the evening. Water evaporates more slowly when it's cool, so more will get to where it's needed, and less will be wasted. You'll also avoid the scorching effect of water droplets on your plants' leaves in strong sunlight.

Use a watering can rather than a sprinkler (229): that way, you can direct water to the base of each of your plants rather than showering your neighbor's driveway. A sprinkler can use more than 150 gallons of water an hour—that's a whopping 1,200 gallons or more if you leave it on overnight. **If you use a hose, fit a trigger nozzle (230)**, so you can shut off the flow when carrying it from one plant to the next.

231 **Easy does it** Wait until the washing machine's full before you do a wash. Each washing cycle uses more than 25 gallons of water, so make sure you're getting the most from every drop.

232 **Comfort blanket** Mulch around your plants each spring when the ground is moist to help stop water from evaporating from the soil's surface and instead get it down to the roots. A layer, at least 3 in. thick, of bark chips, straw, grass clippings, or compost will keep water in, stop sunlight from stimulating weed growth, and add nutrients to the soil.

233 **No jacket required** Install a "tankless" water heater to save as much as 50 percent of the cost of heating your water. These space-saving, highly energy-efficient heaters burn energy only when you need hot water. This eliminates standby heat loss, which can be as high as 3–4 percent every hour for water heaters linked to a storage tank.

234 **Coming around again** Graywater—water that's been used in sinks, bathtubs, showers, or the washing machine—can be used again to flush toilets, or to water the garden if it contains only biodegradable soaps. Some new houses incorporate graywater recycling systems, and they can also be retrofitted.

235 **Bath or shower?** The average bath uses about 20 gallons of water, while the average shower uses about half that. Save water by reserving baths for special occasions.

Of course, showers use less water than baths only if you don't stand under them for too long. **Try to keep your showering time below five minutes (236)**, or you'll be using at least as much water as you would in a bath. An egg-timer suction-cupped onto the shower wall is a good way of keeping track, and makes showering a fun race against time for kids. And **consider installing a hand-held shower (237)**; it directs the water where you want it and wastes less of it.

238 **Pleasant valet Sunday** Next time you reach for the chamois leather, ask yourself whether your car really needs a wash. You might not want your mean machine to suffer the indignity of having "clean me" finger-traced into its grime, but the ritual car cleansing every Sunday morning may be taking things too far the other way.

Besides washing your car less often, try using less water each time. If you **wash your car with a bucket and sponge (239)**, you'll generally use 2–3 gallons of water, whereas using a hose will get you through around 25 gallons. Like your garden, **your car will benefit from being tended to with rainwater (240)** from a rain barrel, which is often softer than tap water and so breaks down dirt and grease more effectively.

If you're not a fan of washing your car yourself, don't despair. Just make sure you **go to a carwash that has installed a water-recycling system (241)**. These can reuse 95 percent of the water from each wash.

242 **Do your plants really need purified drinking water?** Rather than treating your plants to highly processed drinking-quality water from the faucet, consider connecting a rain barrel to the downspout from your roof to collect rainwater, which is actually much better for them.

243 **On flushing** Up to a third of the drinking water that comes into the average Western home goes straight down the toilet, which is a crazy waste of this precious (and highly processed) resource. To reduce the volume per flush, **try putting a plastic bottle filled with water into the cistern (244)**. If you're installing a new bathroom, **specify a dual-flush toilet (245)**, which allows you to choose flush volume according to "load." Finally, and more controversially, **ask yourself whether you really need to flush (246)** every time you use the toilet. Without going into details, just make sure you leave the lid down if you decide not to flush!

247 **Never flush a diaper** Putting a disposable diaper down the toilet unleashes a string of horrors. The absorbent gel they contain is so effective that they can swell enough to block even the broadest of pipes, and meanwhile their bleaching agent seeps into waterways, where it can damage plants, wildlife, and people. Any nappies that make it through the processing system wash up on riverbanks and beaches. So, if you must use them, put them in the trash!

248 **Dump and run** Most college students accumulate piles of possessions that are easier to throw away than take home at the end of the year. Cut down on this waste by selling your stuff at a Dump & Run™ sale. If Dump & Run™ hasn't reached your campus yet, find out how you can set up a sale yourself (see page 371).

249 **PACK YOUR OWN LUNCH** Get yourself a few sturdy containers of different sizes, an unbreakable bottle and/or flask, buy some bulk supplies at the beginning of each week, and let your imagination run wild. With the cash you'll save by not buying heavily packaged convenience foods or eating out, you can afford a different treat every day.

---

250 **Bed baby down naturally** When choosing crib bedding, go for natural fabrics such as cotton, wool, silk, or hemp. These breathable materials help to regulate your baby's body temperature. Choose fabrics that are labeled organic to be sure you're avoiding the chemical pesticide and fertilizer residues present on even "natural" fabrics, which can be absorbed through babies' delicate skin.

251 **Diapers without tears** Use environmentally friendly diaper soak to presoak reusable diapers before washing them using eco-balls (see page 264) for an all-around low-impact baby's bottom.

252 **Spend a day without spending** Every now and then, try to manage without consuming anything bought with money. You may be surprised how easy (and enjoyable!) it is to get by on things you've grown, made, or simply had in your home for ages. If you like to feel part of a movement, join International Buy Nothing Day on the fourth

Thursday of November in the U.S. and Canada, and on the following Saturday in the rest of the world. Leave your wallet at home and see what happens.

253 **Buy some hemp paper** Paper made from hemp uses only a quarter of the land required to produce paper from timber, and the paper is of a much higher quality.

254 **Keep an eye on your food mileage** Each food we buy has clocked up a certain number of "food miles"—the distance it travels from where it was produced to our kitchen. For some exotic or out-of-season fruit and vegetables, their food mileage can run into the thousands. Look at the label to avoid buying these well-traveled luxuries.

255 **Bad business** Think twice before you buy wildlife products, as they could threaten endangered species and even be illegal. Avoid jewelry and other items made from sea turtle shells, elephant ivory, or coral, and if you buy plants such as orchids, cacti, and cycads, make sure they haven't been collected from the wild.

256 **BE A GREEN BOOKWORM** Make sure your thirst for knowledge has a minimal environmental impact by choosing books that are printed on paper that's recycled or from guaranteed sustainable sources (like this one!). If the book you're after isn't available in this form, borrow it from the library instead, and let the publishers know why they've missed out on a sale.

---

257 **Wise up** Environmental issues and innovations are developing at quite a pace. To keep up to date, take out a subscription to a specialist magazine or journal, such as *E* or *The Ecologist*. These titles are available in many different countries, as well as online. If you receive a printed copy, don't forget to circulate it among friends and colleagues—or donate it to your local doctor's office or hairdresser's salon once you've read it.

258 **Cruising along** On long, open stretches of road, cruise control can save fuel by helping your car maintain a steady speed.

259 **Home and dry** While in action, tumble dryers consume more energy than any other household appliance, so if you have one, try to use it only as a last resort, and hang clothes up to dry instead (outside, if possible, to make them smell really fresh). Cutting your tumble-dryer use by just one load a week will reduce your home's CO_2 emissions by around 40 pounds a year. If you have to use the tumble dryer, **keep the filter lint-free (260)** and **run loads back to back while the drum's still hot (261)**.

262 **Headscratcher** Head lice are a common irritation of childhood. But the side effects of chemical lice treatments are potentially a lot worse than irritating—they can include hyperactivity, rashes, and disruption of the immune system. To achieve insect-free tresses the natural way, coat your child's hair in natural hair conditioner, comb through with a wide-tooth comb, and repeat from root to tip with a fine-toothed nit comb to remove the lice. You need to repeat this treatment every couple of days for a week to remove any larvae that may have hatched in the meantime.

263 **Have you got a leaky home?** If you have a water meter, you can detect hidden water leaks by reading it at the beginning and end of a two-hour period when no water is being used. If the two readings are different, there's a leak. Track it down and fix it!

264 **Turn on, tune in, log out** Give someone (perhaps yourself) an MP3 player and a token for some internet downloads. Once they've worked out how to track down their favorite music online, they need never buy another CD—less plastic in the landfill. **Throw in a solar-powered MP3 charger (265)**, and their musical enjoyment can be carbon-neutral from now on.

266 **A priceless gift** In our hectic modern lifestyles, time is often what we value most. If you don't see as much of a good friend as you'd like, instead of buying them a hastily chosen gift that will collect dust or be thrown away, arrange to spend some time with them. It doesn't really matter what you choose to do—it's the opportunity to catch up that's important. And then if you do want to buy them a gift another time, you'll have a better idea what they might like.

267 **Flex your consumer muscles** If you don't like the way certain companies operate—whether the materials or processes they use or the pollution they produce—tell them! Every business depends on you to buy their products or services, and the impacts of consumer action are huge. If organized campaigns aren't your thing, simply **switch your shopping habits (268)**—purchasing power really counts. But you'll have even more impact if you write a polite letter to the company explaining why you're not spending money with them.

269 **Natural mobile** Inspire your baby with a handmade mobile over his or her crib. Instill early memories of natural objects such as driftwood, shells, leaves, and feathers, lovingly collected and tied onto a wooden frame.

270 **That's a wrap** Use recycled wrapping paper to wrap gifts for your loved ones or sew reusable fabric bags. Buy giftwrap and tags made from recycled paper, and use ribbons or string rather than tape, so the paper can be folded up and used again.

271 **Ten thousand steps** Health experts recommend that we walk 10,000 steps a day (roughly equivalent to 5 miles) to maintain good health. Knowing you're keeping your body healthy makes the decision not to drive to the stores much easier. So get yourself a pedometer, and give yourself a small reward each time you exceed this target.

272 **SOAK UP IDEAS** Many traditional cultures live happily and comfortably using a fraction of the resources required to fuel the average Western lifestyle. Look and learn. Try to incorporate some of their natural wisdom into your life.

273 **Keep chemical waste out of waterways** Never pour paints, used oil, cleaning solvents, polishes, pool chemicals, insecticides, and other hazardous household chemicals down drains, sinks, or toilets. Many of these products contain harmful substances, such as petroleum distillates, sodium hypochlorite, ammonia, and formaldehyde, which could end up in nearby water bodies if not disposed of properly. Contact your local sanitation, public works, or environmental health department to find out about hazardous waste collection days and sites. If a local program isn't available, ask for one.

274 **Snap-happy** Taking pictures with a digital camera means you can weed out the blurred shots of your thumb before you waste cash and resources printing them out. However, if you prefer to use a film camera, **choose 36- instead of 24-exposure films (275)** to reduce the price, packaging, and processing chemicals by a third per snap.

276 **Keep the pressure off** Whether or not you have low flow fittings on your faucets and shower, make sure you turn them on only far enough to provide the water you need. Let's face it, you don't need a particularly powerful jet of water to wash your hands or wet a toothbrush.

277 **Help stamp out animal cruelty** If you suspect that an animal is being mistreated—either at home or abroad—report the incident to the Born Free Foundation. Their "travelers' alert" online campaign (see page 373) seeks to bring to justice the perpetrators of animal cruelty and neglect.

278 **Protective sanitary products** The average woman uses 10,000 sanitary products during her lifetime. These tend to be treated with chlorine bleaches, and the dioxins produced are damaging to the environment and to our bodies. **Choose tampons and pads that haven't been bleached with chlorine (279)** and that are made from organic cotton, if possible.

To avoid the need for the vast majority of those 10,000 sanitary products, **try wearing a menstrual cup (280)**. This hygienic bell-shaped silicon container works without leakage or discomfort. It can be washed and reused thousands of times, saving tons of unnecessary waste and a pile of money.

281 **Chock-a-block** Keep your freezer as full as possible: it takes more energy to chill empty space. If you don't need to stock up on food at the moment, empty cardboard boxes will achieve the same result.

282 **Bright lights** Make sure you're getting the full benefit of the energy going into your lights by wiping dust off lighting fixtures and bulbs every few months (make sure that the bulbs are cool first).

283 **A world of toys** Make some toys for your children or help them to come up with their own. Beanbags made from fabric from an old T-shirt stuffed with uncooked lentils, rag dolls made from dresses or shirts, or a dressing-up box filled with hand-me-downs or rummage-sale finds will provide months of fun at little cost and virtually no environmental impact.

284 **Take in a lodger** If you've got a spare room, consider renting it out. Inhabitants of a shared home each use fewer resources than they would if they lived on their own. They also generally save money—and are less likely to suffer from loneliness!

285 **School trip** Offer to help organize a field trip or nature walk for your child's class at school. Experiencing nature firsthand will help to bring any future lessons about the environment to life.

286 **Full steam ahead** If you need to replace your washing machine, look into the latest steam technology. Steam washing machines use 30–40 percent less water and 20 percent less energy than conventional models, can operate without detergent, and leave clothes not only clean but virtually wrinkle-free.

287 **NEW LEASE ON LIFE** Just because you no longer want something doesn't mean it's junk—and it could even make you some money. Try selling unwanted items via the internet (try eBay), donating them to a new owner, or swapping them with neighbors through a community swap shop. These could also be sources of replacement items for yourself.

288 **Dry your dishes naturally** Save energy by switching off your dishwasher before the drying cycle. Open the dishwasher after the final rinse, and the hot dishes will dry quickly on their own.

---

289 **A SENSE OF WONDER** Appreciating nature's diversity can be the first step in developing a caring relationship with our incredible planet. So take your children on a bug foray, stream survey, or birdwatching outing, and try to learn about a few new creatures each time. For an exhilarating overview of the landscape, take your kids on a trip in a hot-air balloon.

---

290 **Minimal lighting** Make sure that any outdoor lights around your home point downward, so they shine light only where it's really needed. Replace halogen lights with low-power compact fluorescent bulbs and switch them on only when they're required.

291 **Put your kettle on the back burner** Fill a Thermos® with water left over when you boil the kettle, and use that for your next few hot drinks, rather than boiling the kettle every time.

292 **Keep them guessing** Strengthen your vegetable garden's resistance to pests by rotating your crops each year. This will help stop pests who are passionate about a particular plant from building up in the soil and surrounding habitats.

293 **Hidden charge** If you leave your cellphone charger plugged in all the time, up to 95 percent of the energy it consumes will go to waste. You can tell that the charger is using electricity because it feels warm. So, always unplug your charger when it's not in use, and **don't leave your phone to charge overnight (294)**—it takes only a couple of hours to get revved up.

Alternatively, **invest in a wind-up phone charger (295)**, which you can use absolutely anywhere. It takes three minutes of charging to power an eight-minute chat, which means keen conversationalists will get very toned forearms!

296 **Pressed for time** When ironing, leave garments that require a cool iron until last. You should be able to turn the iron off and press them flat with the residual heat if you work quickly!

297 **Shutdown routine** Before you leave your desk at the end of the day, take a moment to check that everything's switched off. Leaving your computer on overnight can waste enough energy to laser-print 800 8½ x 11 pages. That adds up to 2,600kWh of energy each year, producing up to 1.9 tons of CO_2, without getting any extra work done!

298 **Grow your own** If you don't have land of your own, find out whether there's a plot available in your local community garden. With a few hours' attention each week, this little patch of land could change the way your family eats, get you super-fit and wean you off supermarket produce aisles for life.

299 **A breath of fresh air** Clear kitchen air naturally by opening the window, rather than using an exhaust fan, which is often ineffective and noisy—and always a waste of energy.

300 **Don't hide heaters** In order to do their work properly, registers and other heaters need to have space to send out their heat, so don't tuck them behind sofas or draperies.

301 **Home economics** Next time you need to buy a stove, look for one that will help you save energy. **Choose a gas model (302)**, if possible, as gas is a more efficient form of energy than electricity, and its operating costs should be half those of a similar electric model. If you don't have a gas supply in your area or space for bottled gas, **find an electric cooker with halogen and induction elements (303)** on the stovetop, which are more efficient than solid disks and radiant elements, and that has a convection oven, which should cut cooking times by up to a third.

However it's powered, **make sure the oven has a glass door and a light (304)** so you can check on your food's progress without needing to open the door and let heat escape.

305 **Pure wool** Although wool is a natural product, the process of producing it is, unfortunately, not as environmentally friendly as the image of a field of fluffy sheep might suggest. Chemicals such as organophosphates used in sheep dip are toxic and potentially carcinogenic, and can leach into water supplies—as can the chlorine used to make wool shrink resistant. So seek out products made from wool produced using organic methods, which avoid such compounds.

306 **Salad days** Turn your back on bagged salad. The "modified atmosphere" packaging designed to preserve the leaves and the chlorine used to wash them combine to destroy valuable antioxidant nutrients, and this intensive processing wastes energy. Instead, **buy a whole lettuce (307)**—it'll be much fresher, and you'll save enough cash to buy some top-quality olive oil for a dressing.

Better still, **grow your own salad greens (308)**. You'll get a decent yield even from a window box. It takes no time, and if you sow in batches every two or three weeks, you'll be making delicious salads for months.

309 **Lucky dip** If you don't live near a farmers' market, subscribing to a weekly delivery from a local farm is a wonderfully easy way of buying fresh organic produce, and is cheaper than buying organic food from stores. You can specify the precise contents of your weekly delivery or ask for a mixed box of whatever happens to be in season—which can be an exciting introduction to unfamiliar types of fruit and vegetables.

To take things further, **consider joining a CSA (Community Supported Agriculture) program (310)**. In return for an annual subscription to a local farm, you'll not only receive a weekly delivery of seasonal produce but also will often be able to participate in the running of the farm and become part of a lively social network of stakeholders.

311 **Wear a hemp shirt** Hemp has been unfairly saddled with a hippie image, which it doesn't deserve. It's a very ecologically friendly crop, which doesn't need pesticides and herbicides to thrive and is now used to make a wide range of fashionable clothes, as well as other products ranging from frisbees to bags.

312 **Stare at a flat screen** Not only do flat LCD (liquid crystal display) screens mean that your TV and computer monitor take up less space (and look snazzier) than the old-fashioned cathode-ray models, they're also much more efficient, using about 30 percent less energy. And because they give off less heat and fewer electronic emissions, your living room or office should be healthier and more comfortable. Just make sure that if you're upgrading, you recycle or donate your old equipment.

313 **Transparent logic** Glass bottles are among the easiest items to recycle. Doing this not only saves resources (1.2 tons of sand, ash, and limestone and 36 gallons of oil for every ton of glass recycled), but also cuts energy use—recycling just one bottle saves enough energy to power a television for 90 minutes.

314 **Give shatoosh shawls the cold shoulder** A fabric of desire for some fashionistas, shatoosh wool is plucked from endangered Tibetan antelopes, which are killed for the purpose. If you covet a super-soft shawl, opt for one made from pashmina wool, which is shaved, leaving the animal intact (if a little chilly).

315 **Put your money where your mouth is** Beware: not all bank accounts are equal. While some banks' investment portfolios might include, for example, the arms industry and tobacco firms and give indirect support to oppressive regimes, others avoid such investments and favor companies with good environmental and humanitarian records. So switch your account to an ethical bank, and let your previous one know why you chose to move on.

316 **Distance no object** If you're tying the knot, first of all, congratulations! Second, ask your guests to let you know how far they'll have to travel to reach the ceremony and what method of transport they'll be using, and invest in an offsetting plan (see page 373) to neutralize the carbon emissions generated.

317 **Lay off the peat** Peat bogs are an ancient and irreplaceable natural habitat, home to a whole host of unique flora and fauna. Unfortunately, they're under threat from human consumption—both for fuel and, primarily, as a base for soil mixes. The best alternative is to produce your own compost, but if you can't make enough for your needs, ask your garden center to stock one of the growing number of brands of peat-free soil mix.

318 **Takeout storage** Plastic takeout containers can be handy boxes for packed lunches or for storing food. Make sure you wash them thoroughly to get rid of any residual spicy odors. However, if you're a takeout fan, you'll quickly accumulate more containers than you can usefully use at home. So **take empty containers back (319)** when you order your next meal, and ask for your food to be served in them, rather than in new boxes. If eyebrows are raised, remind the restaurant that they'll be saving money!

320 **Garden detox** If you've decided to stop using chemical pesticides in your garden, don't chuck the potions still lurking in your shed into the trashcan or down the drain. They could make their way into drinking-water supplies through either route, poisoning ecosystems along the way. Instead, take these substances to a recycling center for safe disposal. Then switch to organic alternatives to avoid the same problems in the future.

321 **Water power** Many large-scale hydroelectric developments, involving the damming of wide valleys, have caused high-profile environmental and social problems, as ecosystems are disrupted and communities displaced. But many countries, from Austria to Nepal, are shifting their focus to smaller-scale hydroelectric projects, which, if responsibly implemented, have relatively small social and environmental impacts, while providing people with power and related economic benefits.

322 **Well preserved** Choose boron- or natural asphalt-based wood preservatives, which penetrate wood without using harmful solvents. The conventional alternatives contain highly toxic nerve poisons and fungicides, which continue to damage the environment for a long time after they've been applied.

323 **Refreshing thought** Use a glass at the water cooler instead of disposable plastic cups or paper cones.

324 **Grow a spud tower** For a bumper harvest from a small space, plant some seed potatoes under a couple of inches of soil mix inside an old tire. When the plants are about 8 in. tall, put another tyre on top and fill with more mix so that only about 2 in. of the growth is left above the surface. You can repeat this process until your tower is four or five tires tall. When buried, the stem becomes root, which sends off potato-producing lateral roots, multiplying the yield from each seed potato.

325 **Join a green gym** Working out on energy-hungry exercise machines in an air-conditioned, windowless box while watching soap operas or rock videos is a strange and often unenjoyable feature of modern life. To get fit in more natural surroundings, look for a volunteer conservation group in your area. These organizations manage environmental projects, such as tree planting and developing school nature areas and public green spaces, which provide the health-giving effects of outdoor exercise while benefiting your community. You can burn up to 30 percent more calories an hour building a footpath than doing aerobics, and you'll learn a lot more skills!

326 BUY LOCAL AND SEASONAL Do you really need to eat mangoes in midwinter if you live in Montana? Resist the supermarket "all-year-round" mentality and get back in tune with local, seasonal produce. You'll reduce the amount of air freight emissions associated with your meal, and support your local farmers.

327 **Ethical aquarium** A fish tank can be a soothing mini-ecosystem in your home or office. But make sure it's not threatening marine populations: stock it with fish that are certified by the Marine Aquarium Council as unendangered species. And **don't buy coral to adorn your tank (328)**, as it's in serious decline in many areas.

329 **WWOOF your way around the world** If you hanker for a change from the beach, why not spend time working on an organic farm during your next vacation? The international WWOOF (World-Wide Opportunities on Organic Farms) association can put you in touch with host farms. This is a great way to encounter places, people, and adventures that are not available to the average tourist.

330 **Wooly lining** If you've had a moth attack in your closet, try using any unsalvageable sweaters or blankets to line a couple of hanging baskets to brighten up your garden in the spring.

331 **Security measure** If you leave a light on when you go away, set it on a timer and make sure you use an energy-efficient bulb.

332 **Organic vacation** Enjoy the benefits of organic produce in beautiful surroundings by staying at one of a growing international network of hotels, guest houses, and farms that specialize in organic hospitality (see page 372).

333 **Green globe** When planning your vacation, try to book with members of Green Globe 21—a worldwide certification program dedicated to helping the travel and tourism industry develop in sustainable ways.

334 **Don't be a water hog on vacation** Water supplies are a particularly acute concern in hot climates. It's easy to squander resources when you're pampering yourself—the average vacationer in Spain, for example, uses twice as much water as each resident. Minimize the impact of your visit by not insisting on a clean towel every day, not bathing more than you would at home, and generally using water carefully.

335 **Dinner time!** Cook a meal from scratch: buy all the ingredients from local sources if you can, and invite your family and friends to help with the cooking—and, of course, the eating.

336 **Smokin'** Firing up the barbecue is a great way to enjoy time outdoors. But make sure the only environmental nuisance caused by your alfresco dining is a waft of savory smoke blowing over the neighbors' garden. **Buy locally sourced charcoal (337)** from a supplier who grows wood sustainably. Avoid charcoal imported from distant places such as Indonesia: it's likely to have come from endangered forests, and to be bulked out with additives such as sand and clay to make it heavier—and therefore more expensive (it's also harder to light).

Don't use lighter fluids or briquettes (338), which are made from gasoline derivatives and can coat your food in harmful deposits. Instead, use some scrunched-up newspaper, dry twigs, and, if necessary, a little kindling (small pieces of wood).

339 **Rocky patch** Rock gardens are great for growing drought-resistant plants and offer shelter to creatures such as frogs, newts, and toads. With this in mind, make sure you incorporate some nooks and crannies in any rock features you build in your garden.

340 **Natural shine** Make your glass and windows cleaner by mixing a little white vinegar in water in a refillable plastic spray bottle. As well as saving money, you'll avoid the isopropyl alcohol contained in most store-bought products. This harms aquatic life and can adversely affect the human nervous system.

341 **Rescue a pet** Instead of buying a pet from a store or breeder, pay a visit to an animal shelter and give a loving home to an animal in need.

342 **Wood is good** When doing carpentry, don't be tempted by composite products such as MDF (medium density fiberboard). Although easy to work, they contain carcinogenic formaldehyde and must be handled with great care. Sustainably forested lumber is your best choice—and in the U.S. there's a plethora of domestic hardwoods and softwoods from which to choose.

343 **The greatest gift** Apply the central environmental principle of "reduce, reuse, recycle" to your own body by agreeing to donate your organs when you die. Carry a donor card, and let your family know your wishes.

344 **Steam-free ironing** When ironing, avoid using the iron's steam setting; instead, spray water onto your clothes using a spray bottle. This greatly reduces your iron's energy use and prevent its workings from clogging up with mineral deposits.

345 **Spray away** Although aerosols no longer contain ozone-munching CFCs, many still use polluting hydrocarbon-based propellants. And since each can is made from a collection of valuable resources that can't be reused or recycled once the contents have been sprayed out, aerosols should be struck from the shopping list of any eco-conscious consumer. They can almost always be replaced with products in reusable pump containers.

346 **A wholesome night's sleep** Next time you need to buy a new mattress, look for one filled with natural materials such as horsehair, cotton, coir, or coconut fiber. They conduct body moisture much more effectively than sweaty synthetic mattresses, don't sag in the middle, and can be produced with a fraction of the environmental impact of fabrics such as nylon. Sleep well!

347 **Computer age** Our growing dependence upon the computer is fast becoming an environmental scourge. More than 31 million PCs are thrown away worldwide each year. The plastic alone in each system requires 7 quarts of crude oil to make, and when computers are discarded many of their components, including lead, nickel, and cadmium, can become environmental hazards. Minimize this wastage by choosing a model that can be easily upgraded. When it's really no longer useful to you, **donate your computer to an organization that recycles IT equipment (348)** for resale or reuse by schools or charities.

349 **Exploratory exercise** Take your children on a bike ride. Besides being a great way to bond with your kids while helping them to get fit, a family bike ride can take you to parts of your neighborhood you'd never have known existed if you'd stayed in your car. Even if there aren't dedicated bicycle lanes on the roads around your home, it's likely there are some bike-friendly trails that will lead you to interesting places. **Ask your national cycling association for maps of recommended routes (350)**.

351 **Impeach the bleach** Besides blitzing the harmful bacteria in your toilet bowl, the caustic soda in bleach-based toilet cleaners kills the valuable organisms needed to digest waste in sewage plants, making the system inefficient and expensive. Instead, look for bleach-free, ecologically friendly toilet cleaners based on natural products. You can also **make your own toilet cleaner (352)**. Flush the toilet to wet the sides, then tip a cup of borax around the bowl, followed by a drizzle of white vinegar. Leave overnight, then scrub with a toilet brush, and flush.

353 **Organic gold mine** More than a third of the waste we put into our garbage cans is compostable organic matter. In a landfill this "green" material breaks down anaerobically to produce methane—a greenhouse gas some 23 times more potent than carbon dioxide. Separating out materials such as vegetable and fruit peel and cardboard packaging gives you free "fuel" for a compost pile, which will generate nutrient-rich matter to condition your soil and nourish your plants.

354 **Hidden menace** The flame retardant PBDE is often used to treat furniture, carpets, and clothes. This very persistent synthetic compound accumulates in our bodies and has been linked to hormone dysfunction. Make retailers aware of your desire to avoid this compound by asking for PBDE-free products.

355 **Up, up, and away** Use natural latex balloons to adorn your children's parties. A bunch of balloons drifting into the blue yonder can be a pretty spectacle, but once they've landed, the burst bubbles of foil or treated latex will linger as litter for years, and can choke cattle and wildlife. Natural latex is fully biodegradable—even if the occasional balloon does end up in a tree rather than your compost pile.

356 **Dust to dust** Cremation releases a cocktail of toxins into the air. So opt for burial if you can, ideally in a woodland or farmland site, where your remains will nourish the earth you came from.

357 **Wedding list** Ask your friends and family to help set you up for a low-impact married life with gifts such as organic bed linen, solar-powered appliances or maybe even a mini wind turbine.

358 **Write an ethical will** Keep up your good work after you're gone by making a will that helps future generations look after the planet (see page 371). Leave bequests to organizations or charities you trust to make a difference on your behalf.

359 **Shattering success** The satisfying crash of glass being thrown into a glass-recycling container can be a great stress buster. But before you chuck those bottles, make sure that you've got them sorted by color, if this is required by your local recycling program. Otherwise, it will all be used to make green glass, which is of a lower value than other colors.

360 **Does it work on bee stings?** Manuka honey has great antiseptic qualities—try using it to clean and soothe minor cuts, burns, and grazes without the need for harsh chemical creams.

361 **Give a recycled gift** Give a friend something beautiful or unusual made from recycled materials, such as a piece of jewelry or clothing, to remind them that there's more to recycled products than just toilet paper.

362 **Caring confetti** Rosebuds, petals, blossom, or biodegradable confetti made from recycled tissue paper bring magic to a just-married moment, then dissolve quickly.

---

363 **HOUSE AN OWL** Barn owls like to nest in hollow trees or hidden corners of old buildings. If you own a large garden, make it owl-friendly: install nesting boxes under the eaves of your home, leave old trees standing, and keep an area of grass uncut to provide a habitat for the small rodents on which owls prey.

---

364 **Mug's game** Keep a mug at work for all the hot drinks you need to fuel your day. You're a busy person—you deserve better than a mouthful of polystyrene or plastic.

365 **Over and over** Buy rewritable CDs and DVDs for files you need to copy or transport. If looked after properly, these disks can be reused hundreds of times, avoiding the need to buy packs and packs of single-use equivalents. Alternatively, **use a USB flash drive or your MP3 player (366)** to transport files.

367 **Take the easy option** Suggest to your employer that recycling containers (particularly for paper) be put closer to people's desks than the normal wastebaskets, so that even in the flurry of meeting a deadline, recycling's the easier option.

368 **Permanent marker** Find a fountain pen you love, and use it for life. A refillable pen with a nib that suits your writing style will make writing a more pleasant (and stylish) experience and will avoid the waste of throwing out dozens of pens every year.

For scribbles when your fountain pen's not appropriate, **choose a mechanical pencil or refillable ballpoint pen (369)**.

370 **Windows across the world** Next time you have a short meeting in a far-flung location, ask yourself whether you really need to be there in person. Video conferencing could save you a lot of time and avoids environmentally damaging travel.

371 **Buy for keeps** Take advantage of low prices during the sales to invest in a few items you really need and want but that are normally outside your budget. A high-quality piece of clothing or furniture will last many times longer than a cheaper alternative.

372 **Respect your plastics** Despite its environmental problems, plastic can be very useful, and is impossible to avoid entirely in modern life. Make sure you're getting the most out of this valuable resource by reusing plastic packaging, then recycling it when it's no longer usable. Look for items made from PETE (marked with a number 1 inside a triangle), which is the most easily recyclable plastic. Recycling just one PETE bottle saves enough energy to power a 60-watt lightbulb for six hours.

373 **Tired eyes?** Before you buy another beauty elixir claiming to restore your natural sparkle, try putting the following on your closed eyes: cool wet tea bags (black, green, chamomile, elderflower, catnip, and lavender tea are all soothing), cucumber slices, or cotton puffs dampened with witch hazel. Lie down and relax for at least ten minutes to let the natural compounds do their stuff. If nothing else, you'll feel more rested.

374 **Go the extra mile** If you're going to the effort of saving bottles for recycling, make sure you first remove caps, corks, and other additions, which contaminate potentially useful glass.

375 **THE GRASS IS GREENER** A gasoline-powered mower can produce as much pollution per hour as 40 cars! Instead, use an electric mower (ideally powered by electricity from a green supplier)—or a manual reel mower, which will get you fit while you push it. Technogardeners could go for self-guiding solar-powered models.

376 **Working lunch** Get together with colleagues to make food at lunchtime or have a pot luck, and enjoy bonding with them over something more substantial than coffee. If necessary, ask your employer to provide basic facilities for food preparation, so you don't have to rely on convenience food in disposable packaging.

377 **Circular argument** No matter how shining your prose may be, there's no need to use brand-new envelopes to circulate internal notes and memos. Keep a supply of used envelopes on hand, and ask your colleagues to do the same.

378 **Eco poop scoop** To avoid adding to the plastic-bag mountain, scoop dog poop with bags made from biodegradable cornstarch instead—these are available from many pet shops.

379 **Make love, not pollution** When you've released yourself from Eros's embrace, don't throw your condom down the toilet, or it'll clog water-treatment facilities, or could end up on a riverbank or beach. Instead, choose biodegradable latex condoms (most condoms are made of polyurethane) and put them in the trash afterward.

380 **Can the cans** From canned pet food, gradually switch your dog or cat's diet to dried foods packaged in large cardboard or paper containers. They're lighter, saving on transportation costs and energy use, and the packaging is less resource- and energy-intensive (and can be added to your compost pile).

381 **Cool for cats** Conventional cat litter is based on clay or other minerals—products of environmentally damaging mining, and a heavy toxic burden in landfill sites once discarded. If your cat has no outdoor access and really needs a litter tray, try biodegradable alternatives made of sawmill wastes, straw, or hemp. They're lighter and can be flushed away or, preferably, buried in the soil of your garden.

382 **Use the right rocks** If you're planning a rock garden, use local stone. Transporting stone from distant areas is a waste of energy; and local stone will look more natural in your garden anyway. Ideally, use rocks dug from your own land or rejects from local building sites. If you do need to purchase stones, make sure they haven't been taken from an area where they're in short supply. On a cumulative scale, such removal can damage rare habitats.

383 **Rag trade** Just because some of your oldest clothes are too worn out to be useful to anyone in their current incarnation, they needn't be discarded. Some charities are becoming increasingly adept at fashioning new items out of the best parts of unwanted old garments. And if your togs are beyond even that, they can still be shredded and rewoven into new items, via a charity-run textile recycling program.

384 **On the piste** If you're a skiing fan, make sure your enjoyment of the slopes is of minimal threat to mountain areas—already suffering the early effects of climate change—by choosing a ski resort that's taking steps to minimize its environmental impact (see page 372). Initiatives to look for include wind-powered ski lifts and car-pooling for staff and guests.

385 **Out in the cold** Write to refrigerator manufacturers to urge them to adopt "greenfreeze" technology, which cools using butane and propane rather than the ozone-munching CFCs, HFCs, or HCFCs, and tends to be more energy-efficient. "Greenfreeze" fridges are popular in many parts of the world, but U.S. manufacturers have, so far, resisted making the change.

386 **Make your own logs** Turn your newspapers into heating fuel using a "log maker"—a small gadget, available online, that turns your reading matter into compact pulp. Each newspaper will make roughly one log, which will burn for up to an hour. You can feed some versions of this device with paper shreddings, cardboard, wood chips, dry leaves, twigs, chopped branches, wrapping paper, and junk mail. More simply, **roll newspaper sheets around a broomstick (387)** until the "log" is the desired thickness, then soak it thoroughly in water. Dry the log overnight, remove the broomstick, and use it like ordinary wood.

388 **Low-cost reading** Do you really need to pay through the nose for every word you read? Newspapers and magazines tend to be read only once before they're thrown away. Try cutting down your weekly reading stack by listening to the news on the radio, reading online, or browsing the freebies in cafés and libraries.

389 **Cut out the legwork** If you're looking for an out-of-print book, save yourself wasted (and wasteful) journeys to secondhand bookstores by visiting a website (see page 371) that allows you to search a global network of book dealers.

390 **Career change** If your old clothes, sheets, and towels are too worn out to grace a thrift shop, try cutting them into squares to use as washable cloths for cleaning floors and other surfaces, dusting, and wiping up spills.

391 **DO A HOME DRAFT AUDIT** Hold a lit candle next to window and door frames. If the flame flickers, there's a gap that needs to be plugged.

392 **Better battery habits** Most batteries leak toxic metals such as mercury, nickel and cadmium when you throw them away. So choose rechargeable alkaline manganese batteries, which are free from toxic heavy metals, invest in a battery charger (ideally, a solar-powered one), and teach everyone in your family how to use it.

393 **Faithful friend** Exotic pets are often captured from endangered wild populations and imported illegally. They can be hard to care for and so often end up dumped in the wild, where they can wreak havoc on the local ecosystem. Build a more lasting relationship with a dog or cat from your local animal shelter.

394 **Definitely not cool** Dumped fridges and freezers are not only an eyesore but an ecological hazard, as they can contain ozone-depleting CFCs and HCFCs. At the end of your appliance's life, take it to a dedicated recycling point, where these chemicals can be professionally removed.

395 **Elect to vote** It can often feel like we have little say over the way our world is run. But if you live in a democracy, your vote counts! At election time, find out which candidate is offering the best deal for the planet, and give them your support. Better still, contact your local political representative right now and let them know what you'd like them to do on your behalf.

396 **Don't be foiled** Aluminum production is a resource- and energy-intensive process. So use foil sparingly; and, where possible, wash and fold it for reuse. When it's no longer usable, make sure you recycle it.

When there's no option but to use aluminum foil (for example, for covering food while roasting), make sure you **use a foil made from 100 percent recycled aluminum (397)**. Recycling aluminum uses a twentieth of the energy needed to smelt the virgin metal from ore.

398 **Veggie vacation** If you'd like to eat more vegetarian meals but are stuck for inspiration, why not put yourself in the hands of some experts on a course, tour, or even vacation focused on vegetarian or vegan food (see page 372)? As well as giving you all kinds of appetizing recipe ideas, they'll show you how to derive the full range of nutrients from a plant-based diet.

399 **Pond life** Make a pond in your garden and create a whole new ecosystem right on your doorstep. Make sure it has gently sloping sides to enable small animals to escape if they fall in (and a fence around it if you have small children). A combination

of shallow and deep areas planted with a mix of aquatic plants will provide habitats for a range of creatures, who'll quickly colonize their new home if it's left undisturbed for a few months.

400 **Happy re-tire-ment** When they're no longer roadworthy, old tires can be turned into new products, such as safe surfaces for playgrounds, mouse mats, or notebook covers. Support this reuse industry by buying a tire-based gift for a car-mad friend.

401 **Comfort food** When you've finished using your oven, open the door and let the warm air help heat your home.

402 **Crafty wrapping** Use up scraps of material from curtain- or dress-making or old unwanted clothes to make a beautiful, personalized bag to wrap a gift. If it's well made, it may last longer than the gift inside! Perhaps even cannier, **look for "wrapping" that's a gift in itself (403)**, such as a brightly colored dish towel or scarf, or a beautiful storage box. These can all contain smaller gifts and will be treasured in their own right. Add a (reusable) ribbon to perfect the waste-free presentation of your gift.

404 **Fact of life** Your one cat might not have much of an environmental impact, but if it produced even a couple of litters, it could end up at the head of a feline family tree of thousands, which would make a severe dent in the local population of small creatures. Do the responsible thing: get your cat neutered.

405 **Outdoor education** Encourage your local school to establish a conservation area in its grounds. This could simply be an area of land left to regenerate into a variety of natural habitats, or a more diverse patch incorporating a working garden. Either way, it will be an important teaching resource. Offer your time to help establish and manage it.

406 **Get behind the bike shelter** In Denmark 60 percent of children cycle to school. Encourage your local school to move toward this target by asking them to provide secure bike shelters for pupils and staff.

407 **Reinvent the wheel** In Los Angeles County alone, some 10 million tires are discarded every year—and they take up to 400 years to begin decomposing. Help to reduce this rubber mountain by retreading your tires when they wear down. This process is carried out to strict safety standards and uses only a fraction of the energy it takes to replace the tire.

If your car does need new "shoes," ask your garage to **fit eco-friendly tires (408)**, which use organic ingredients such as cornstarch in place of non-renewable chemicals.

409 Good news about hydrogen Many experts believe that hydrogen will play a key role in building a diversified energy system based on renewable power supplies, as it can be used as a medium for carrying and storing energy. This could help even out the intermittency of some renewable sources—for example, enabling energy from sunlight to be stored for use overnight.

Major automobile manufacturers are developing vehicles with electric motors powered by hydrogen fuel cells. This technology has the potential to drastically reduce pollution: the only thing that comes out of the tailpipe of a hydrogen car is water vapor.

At the moment, the most efficient way to produce hydrogen is by burning natural gas, a fossil fuel. However, scientists are working hard to find a way to enable large-scale production using renewable energy. Keep up with the latest developments.

410 **Traffic filter** Traveling along the side of the road, cyclists are actually exposed to two to four times less pollution than people inside vehicles stuck bumper to bumper in a traffic jam. But to give added protection to your lungs while cycling, get yourself a face mask to cover your nose and mouth.

---

411 **SOMETHING FOR NOTHING** Look for gadgets such as radios and chargers—for everything from phones to laptops—that run on solar power and/or wind-up mechanisms.

---

412 **Pool your resources** If everyone who regularly drives to work on their own were to share a ride with a neighbor or colleague even just once a week, traffic volumes would fall by 10–15 percent.

413 **Two-mile rule** Up to half of journeys made by car in developed countries are less than two miles long. Sadly, this is when car engines are at their least efficient and most polluting. Make it a rule to walk or cycle journeys of less than two miles. You may need to invest in some waterproof clothing and decent walking shoes, but your legs and heart will thank you in the long run.

If you're not sure that your legs can cope with regular cycling, **try an electric bicycle (414)** instead. Quiet and clean (especially if powered using renewable energy), it lets you glide through traffic at speeds of up to 15 miles an hour. If storage space is your problem, at home or at work, **buy a folding bicycle (415)**.

416 **Take great strides** Try strapping some springy "powerizer" stilts onto your calves to increase your stride length dramatically. Once you've mastered the rocking motion, you'll be able to leap forward around 15 feet with a single bound, enabling you to make journeys on foot in a fraction of the usual time.

417 **Take a meal on the wild side** You may be surprised how much food is growing all around you. If you're uncertain what to look for, carry a good identification guide to the wild plants in your region. Select young, fresh plants from unpolluted areas, and don't take more than will quickly grow back. You could try making wild garlic pesto, elderflower wine, blackberry jam, nettle soup, crab apple jelly, horseradish sauce, or sage tea . . . Your food will be guaranteed free from pesticides and preservatives—fresh and very local.

418 **Flushed with excess** There's no good reason for using a 1- or 2-gallon flush of carefully processed drinking water to dispose of anything that could go into your trashcan, recycling container, or compost pile. Apart from the terrible waste of a precious resource, when flushed down the toilet items such as tampons, condoms, and razor blades can cause blockages in the sewage system and end up in waterways or on the beach. Wouldn't you rather feel sand between your toes?

419 **Recycle your cycle** If you're upgrading your bike, don't scrap the old one. Your local bike store may offer a part-exchange plan, and even if your bike's too much of a wreck to be of any value to them, it's still likely to be useful for parts. Bicycle recycling programs are often community run and provide jobs for people out of work. Some projects collect, mend, and ship secondhand bicycles and parts to Africa (see page 371).

420 **Make the plastic bag history** We use 8 percent of the world's oil supply to produce plastic, including billions of plastic bags each year. Not only is this a huge waste of resources, but it results in lots of unnecessary long-term landfill, as it's believed that each bag will take up to 500 years to decompose. When you do get a plastic bag from a store, stash it away for reusing later. **Ask stores that use plastic bags to provide biodegradable ones (421)** made from cornstarch. Better yet, **take a shopping bag with you (422)**; keep one or two in the car to be used as needed. This will also help you to cut down on the number of paper bags you acquire.

423 Relabel your envelopes Instead of throwing all the envelopes you receive away after a single use, open them carefully so they can be reused by sticking a label over the original address. Buy some self-adhesive labels (made from recycled paper) that are large enough to fold over the top of the envelope, so that you don't need any tape or staples to seal it.

424 Make some lemonade Grow your own lemons—by planting a citrus tree in your yard or keeping a potted Meyer lemon tree indoors—and mix the juice from them with some sugar and filtered water to make a drink that's cheaper, more healthful, and much, much tastier than lemon-flavored soda.

425 **Plant a wildflower meadow** Instead of having a large, manicured lawn, try planting an area of your garden with a wildflower mix. Wildflower meadows grow best on poor soil, so don't require any fertilizers (or weedkillers, of course), need cutting only twice a year, are gorgeously colorful, and attract butterflies, birds, and bees.

426 In praise of jute Otherwise known as burlap, the fibrous plant jute needs far less water than cotton and little or no fertilizer and pesticide. It has many uses—from reusable carrier bags to curtains, carpets, and matting to prevent soil erosion.

427 Chop on wood So-called "antibacterial" plastic chopping boards have become popular in recent years. But there is concern that the triclosan impregnated in these and similar household products can foster antibiotic-resistant strains of bacteria. There's no need to introduce this potentially risky substance into your home. Far better to harness the natural bactericidal properties of wood: a regularly scrubbed, sustainably sourced wooden chopping board can't be beaten.

428 Don't be a butthead Once you've stubbed out your cigarette, make sure you put it in a trashcan. Besides being an eyesore, these tiny pieces of litter can choke birds and animals, or poison them with tobacco and tar if they manage to swallow them.

429 Open and shut case Line your drawers beautifully using unused ends of wallpaper rolls.

430 Festive glow Christmas lights aren't the most essential way to use energy, but the festive period would be far duller without them. To get the most striking effect for the least electricity, **try hanging LED (Light Emitting Diode) lights (431)**. These 0.4-watt bulbs use up to 100 times less energy than some traditional Christmas lights, and last up to 100,000 hours when used indoors. And, unlike some of the energy-hungry conventional versions, if one of the LED lights burns out, the rest of the strand will stay lit, meaning that there's never a problem identifying the faulty bulb.

Decorative lights designed for indoors generally use less energy than outdoor versions, so if you want to share your festive spirit with your neighbors, **string lights around the inside of your windows (432)** rather than outside.

433 Show your cans who's boss Recycling just one aluminum can saves enough energy to run a TV set for three hours. Help make the process even more efficient by crushing your cans before collection. This means that they take up less space, which reduces the number of trips required to take them to the recycling plant. (The same principle applies to plastic bottles.)

Crushing cans with your own strength is a great way to release frustration (as long as you take care with sharp edges), but you can also **get a can crusher (434)**—a simple gadget that makes short work of even the sturdiest cans.

435 **Get going!** Drive off as soon as you start your car's engine. Modern engines don't need time to warm up, so idling creates unnecessary pollution and mechanical wear.

436 **Be an anti-litter bug** Pick up at least one piece of litter each day and put it in a trashcan (or recycle it if appropriate). This might seem like an inconsequential action, but if everyone on your street did the same, there would be dumpsterloads less litter blowing around your front door.

437 **Never pour engine oil down the drain!** Instead, ask your local gas station or recycling center whether they accept it for re-refining. This process filters out toxic heavy metals such as nickel, cadmium, and lead and leaves the oil as good as new (see pages 270–271). A single gallon of oil poured down the drain can contaminate millions of gallons of water.

438 **TAKE YOUR CHILDREN TO AN ORGANIC FARM** Some organic farms encourage visitors to explore their land on nature trails or simply to look and learn. There should be plenty to spot—in addition to the obvious crops and herds, one British study has shown that organic farms contain 85 percent more plant species, 33 percent more bats, 17 percent more spiders, and 5 percent more birds than nonorganic ones.

---

439 **Buy recycled stationery** Recycled paper not only saves trees but requires a lot less energy to produce than virgin paper. It's also free from chlorine-based bleach and petrochemical-based optical brighteners, which, when they enter waterways, can damage plants and animals.

440 **Invest in an eco-friendly pension fund** You'll get old a lot more gracefully if you retire ethically. Make sure that your monthly payments are funding something positive by choosing a fund that invests according to stringent eco-friendly criteria.

441 Buy an acre of rain forest Tropical rain forests are the Earth's oldest and most complex land-based ecosystem and contain half of its wildlife and at least two-thirds of its plant species. They play a key role in regulating global climate and preventing soil erosion, are home to indigenous cultures, and provide a rich source of ingredients for medicines. But an area the size of Massachusetts is being cut down every year in the Amazon alone to make way for cattle ranching, logging, plantations, mining, oil exploration, and dams. Do your bit by "buying" a section of this vital ecosystem (see page 370) to ensure it's protected in perpetuity.

442 High-IQ battery charging Some chargers continue to feed energy into batteries even when they're fully charged. To avoid wasting energy and reducing battery life by overcharging, look for an "intelligent" charger that uses the "delta v" or "delta t" detection technique to sense when charging is complete and then reduces its energy output to a trickle. That way you don't have to be around to unplug it once your battery is charged.

443 Clean, hot cooktop If you have an electric cooktop, clean it regularly so that the rings can work efficiently.

444 **Polar bear necessities** Warmer temperatures in the Arctic could soon make polar bears a creature of the past. As the cold season becomes shorter, the ice the bears hunt on is frozen for shorter periods each year, giving them less time to build up the fat reserves they need to live on for the rest of the year. Help to protect these beautiful creatures by taking as many actions as you can to limit your contribution to climate change.

445 **A simpler life** If you want to reduce your impact on the world, concentrate on simplifying your life (see page 373). Make an effort to reduce the number of things you own, keeping only belongings that you use or enjoy regularly and passing on others to those who can use them. This will probably feel difficult to begin with, but by developing this mindset, you'll naturally buy less and create less waste in the future.

446 **Foster an ape** Our closest relatives, the apes, are under increasing threat as we hunt them and plunder their habitats. By joining a fostering program, you can support charities that look after the orphans found wandering when their mothers have been killed for food or taken for the illegal pet trade.

447 **Take your time** Rushing often makes "convenience" options unavoidable—jumping into a taxi, rather than walking to a meeting, or grabbing a packaged sandwich, rather than eating fresh food for lunch. This hectic approach often carries a hefty price tag—both for our wallets and the environment—and can be detrimental to our health and happiness. Plan ahead as much as you can, and be realistic about how much you can fit into the day. You may have to do less. But try to do it properly—and enjoy the ride!

448 **Be a fruit and veggie traditionalist** Always favoring the most productive and disease-resistant option, most supermarkets stock a tiny selection of the huge range of fruit and vegetable varieties traditionally grown. About 90 percent of lettuce and 80 percent of tomato varieties have been lost in this focus on profitability, depriving us of a host of wonderful flavors and limiting the biological diversity which allows crops to adapt naturally to cope with changing growing conditions. Buck the trend, and tantalize your tastebuds by buying and growing as many different types of fruit and vegetable as you can.

449 **How big is your footprint?** Work through an ecological footprint quiz (see page 370) to estimate how much productive land and water is used to support your lifestyle, and see how that compares to people in other parts of the world. You may find that you're already living quite lightly, but you're more likely to get a shock—if everyone on Earth lived like the average Westerner, we'd need more than three planets to support us.

---

450 **WALK YOUR TALK** Don't just talk about changing the world—get on with it! Actions speak louder than words. As Mahatma Gandhi said, we must "be the change we want to see in the world."

---

451 **The sea is not a garbage can** The oceans may be vast, but they're becoming clogged with our trash. Much of the waste we produce takes centuries to break down and causes untold environmental damage in the process. Explain to your children—if they don't know already—that throwing trash off a boat or a pier is just as bad as dropping it in the street.

452 **Outward bound** Host your child's birthday party in the woods. Challenge the unruly mob to make dens that will shelter them from the elements. Tap into their animal instincts, and watch them become absorbed in the natural world around them.

453 **Birdwatching** Survey the birds in your yard: put a range of foods on a bird table, and spend ten minutes (or longer, if you like) each day counting how many birds visit in that period. As you make your yard more attractive to different species and put food out more regularly, you should notice an increase in the number of feathered visitors. A basic identification book will help you work out who's who.

454 **Make your own popcorn** Heat a little oil in a large pan. Once the oil is hot, cover the bottom of the pan with a thin layer of corn kernels and put a lid on. Shake the pan from time to time to stop the kernels from burning, and take it off the heat once the popping sounds have subsided. Add a little salt or sugar for a cheap, low-impact snack that's more healthful than heavily packaged, additive-laced commercial equivalents.

455 **Feeling clucky?** If you have a little outdoor space, it's very easy to keep a few chickens to provide you with daily eggs. They eat almost anything except citrus peel, so you can feed them all your kitchen scraps, making sure they get a nutritious (organic if you're eating it), and hormone-free diet that will be recycled into delicious, fresh, food-mile-free (see page 90) eggs for you and your family. As an added benefit, chickens enjoy foraging for numerous garden pests, including slugs and snails.

456 **Natural deodorant** Many commercial deodorants contain aluminum, which can be absorbed through the skin, affect internal organs, and increase the risk of blood poisoning. They also tend to be highly perfumed and packaged. Instead, go for a natural "crystal" deodorant made from mineral salts. One of these lasts for years, so minimizing packaging and transportation. Or for a homemade alternative, **try patting bicarbonate of soda onto damp skin after washing (457)**.

458 **Clean, green shaving** The average (cleanshaven) man spends five months of his life shaving. So make sure this time-consuming ritual has minimal environmental impact: first

of all by choosing a razor that requires you to replace only the blade head when the blade gets blunt, not the whole body of the razor. **Use a razor-cartridge sharpener (459)** to extend the life of your blade: this will reduce the number of disposable blade heads you get through by up to 75 percent. Even better, **shave the old-fashioned way (460)** with a straight razor and hard soap. The blades are permanent and offer the closest shave, and a good vegetable-based soap is better for the environment.

If the cutthroat route seems too daunting, **try a rechargeable electric razor (461)**, which, aside from its potentially toxic hardware makeup, is by no means the worst option. A good model can last for years and provides a close shave without highly packaged and processed creams or gels.

---

462 **DRAFT-DODGING** Stop heat from sneaking out, and make your home more comfortable by fixing weatherstripping (either foam or longer-lasting metal strips) around doors, windows and mail slots. Plug any gaps between baseboards and the floor with base molding.

463 **Down in the basement** If you have a cellar, installing a layer of underfloor insulation will cut heat loss from your home by up to a quarter and will create a much cozier basement.

464 **Get off the treadmill** Exercise machines burn up an enormous amount of electricity (ten treadmills in the average gym use enough electricity each month to run a hair dryer nonstop for more than a year), and the gyms that house them are also heavy consumers of air conditioning and laundry. So put your gym membership on hold, and go for a run in the park instead—or burn some carbs in the real-world gym (see pages 332–333).

465 **Vintage style** The quality of workmanship on vintage clothes is often much higher than on modern mass-produced clothing, so not only will classic clothing generally cost less, it'll also last longer than new items. And your style will be unique!

466 **The answer, my friend** Wind power is now generating electricity in more than 40 countries worldwide and production capacity has grown by nearly 30 percent per year over the past decade. As well as buying in energy from large-scale wind farms, householders can generate their own wind power by installing a wind turbine (typically 6 ft. in diameter) on the roof. This solves the problem of loss of energy in transmission over long distances. In average wind conditions, a domestic turbine could cut your electricity bill by a third. Alternatively, to share setup costs and maximize generation potential, talk to your local government about establishing a community wind farm (see page 371).

467 **Love your bling?** To help avoid the environmental problems associated with mining metal and gems, buy jewelry made from recycled precious metals and stones, or dust off old pieces handed down by your grandparents—perhaps commissioning a jeweler to transform them into radiant recycled classics.

468 **Reincarnate your cellphone** Improved technology and increasingly fashionable and appealing designs mean we update our cellphones ever more regularly. The discarded old ones can leach a cocktail of environmentally damaging metals and flame retardants into the air and groundwater. So be sure either to return the old phone to your retailer for recycling or donate it to a charity that collects them for reuse.

469 **No smoke without fire** Avoid burning trash in your yard: it can release clouds of harmful chemicals and carbon dioxide. Limit bonfires to wood, leaves, and other organic waste if you really can't keep your hands out of the matchbox. But it's much easier and more beneficial to dispose of organic matter on a compost pile.

470 **Count the calories** You may be used to thinking about the amount of energy, or calories, that the food you eat provides you with. But have you thought about how much energy goes into growing and processing your food? The toll can quickly add up—modern food production and distribution systems can use up to 15 times more energy than the resulting food actually provides you with. To cut the production calories, try to buy as many fresh, unprocessed foods as possible.

471 **Greenhouse effect** You can make mini-greenhouses out of plastic bottles. Simply cut off the base, and use the remaining "cloche" as a starter home for seedlings. It'll create a warm microclimate, and keep slugs and snails at bay through the plants' early months.

472 **KEEP THE PRESSURE UP** Maintaining the appropriate pressure in your vehicle's tires will help to minimize its fuel use.

---

473 **Bring dead wood back to life** Instead of sending waste wood from your yard to landfill, try breaking it into small pieces and adding it to your compost pile, where it will provide valuable fiber.

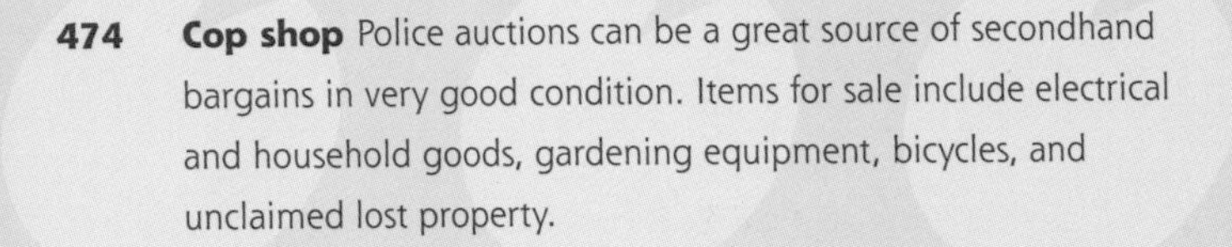

474 **Cop shop** Police auctions can be a great source of secondhand bargains in very good condition. Items for sale include electrical and household goods, gardening equipment, bicycles, and unclaimed lost property.

475 **Bricks work** Keep hold of old bricks: they have many uses in the garden—from supporting a rain barrel or planter to making a raised bed or barbecue stand.

476 **Hot spot** Try to position your compost pile in a sunny spot. The warmer it is, the faster the micro-organisms it contains will do their work. Just make sure you turn the composting material over regularly, especially in very hot weather, to keep it evenly damp and aerated.

477 **Make a mini-pool** If you haven't got space for a pond, try filling a container, such as an old enamel or ceramic sink, with water and putting it in a quiet place in your garden. Add a few stones at one end, so that frogs, toads, and other creatures can get in and out easily.

478 **Keep pests at bay** When faced with insects in your kitchen, instead of resorting to a store-bought chemical solution that's dangerous to children and the environment, try some natural alternatives. Many insects have an aversion to basil; ants don't like cucumber peel or peppermint; and weevils can be kept out of your flour and cereals by adding bay leaves.

479 **Save your candles for next year, and the one after . . .** Birthday cakes with candles aren't a serious contributor to climate change—even if you're celebrating a hundredth birthday with the right number of candles. But to save space at the landfill, blow out the candles and reuse them next time, with their tops cut off. On a green planet maybe we'll all live to be a hundred.

480 **Drain-busting** Clear your drains with a mixture of baking soda and vinegar in boiling water, using a plunger for extra power. This solution is much cheaper than commercial drain cleaners, which contain corrosive and toxic ingredients, such as sodium hydroxide, hydrochloric acid, and petroleum distillates, which damage aquatic life and make water more expensive to treat.

481 **Keep a weather eye** Before you water the garden, check the local weather forecast. If rain's in the offing, there's no need to give your plants a drink, so override your automatic irrigation.

482 **Shine on** To give silverware a natural polish, put a sheet of aluminum foil into a plastic or glass bowl. Sprinkle with salt and baking soda, and fill the bowl with warm water. Soak your silver items in the bowl, and the tarnish will migrate to the foil. Dry and buff your treasures, and they're ready for use, with no nasty chemical residues to spoil the flavor of your next family meal.

483 **Brass rubbing** Polish brass fittings the natural way by rubbing them with half a lemon sprinkled with salt. Let the metal dry, and then buff it with a cloth.

484 **Strike a light!** One of the simplest ways to get rid of a bad smell—in the bathroom, for example—is to strike a match and let the flame burn for a moment. This miraculously eliminates nasty odors without the need to mask them with another, often highly packaged and processed scent. Just make sure you extinguish the match properly before you put it in the wastebasket!

485 **CREDIT-WORTHY** Do some good every time you flex your plastic by using an affinity-type credit card (see page 371) that makes a small donation to a charity every time you use it. Even better, do this good work yourself: **look for ways to reduce unnecessary spending (486)**, and give a proportion of the money you save directly to charity.

487 **Let's hear it for latex paint**

Because they're water-based, latex paints contain fewer hazardous chemicals than oil-based paints, and don't require dangerous solvents for thinning or brush cleaning. They perform at least as well as their oil-based equivalents for most indoor and outdoor jobs.

488 **Recycle leftover paint** If you've got various cans of leftover paint, mix them together to make a primer for your next paint job. But don't try to combine different types (such as latex and oil-based paints), or you'll end up with an unusable gunk.

489 **Love your brushes** Take care of your paintbrushes and they'll last much longer. Buy good-quality brushes and clean them carefully. When you've finished painting, first wipe any excess paint onto newspaper. Then, for oil brushes, use a small amount of turpentine, and wipe with more newspaper. For latex brushes, use hot water and a spot of detergent. Keep brushes used for black paint just for black paint jobs.

490 **Preparation is all** Calculate the surface area to be painted before you start decorating, so you buy only as much paint as you need to cover it.

491 **Hook your carpets down** If you're having new wall-to-wall carpets fitted, ask the fitter to use physical fastening "hook and loop" strips or dry adhesives like peel-and-stick strips rather than commercial adhesives, which can be a major source of harmful volatile organic compounds (see page 186).

492 **Buy reclaimed wooden furniture** An area of ancient woodland the size of a football field is destroyed every two seconds. Make sure your home isn't contributing to the destruction by buying furniture that's either secondhand or made from reclaimed wood.

493 **Look for leaks** A significant proportion of the water processed for human use is lost before it reaches our homes and offices. Help your water company get on top of this problem by reporting any leaks or unusual puddles. And play your part by fixing any leaking pipes in and around your own home.

494 **Foods of love** The sustainable methods used to farm oysters make this aphrodisiac one of the most environmentally sound, so go ahead and indulge yourself. **Stay in the mood with other eco-friendly products (495)** such as ginkgo biloba, believed to help with impotence, and ginseng, said to boost stamina.

---

496 GET TO KNOW YOUR LOWLIFE NEIGHBORS

To show your children just how many creatures share your garden, sink a clean jam jar, with its lid off, into a hole in the ground, and leave it out on a warm, dry night. Next morning, introduce your kids to the beetles, woodlice, and other tiny creatures who've stumbled in, before tipping them out to resume their business.

---

497 **Office clear-out?** Every corporate revamp releases a stream of perfectly serviceable desks, filing cabinets, and other office furniture that may well be gold dust to community groups, churches, shelters, or schools. So ask if they'd like some new equipment before it all goes to the dump.

498 Keep on keeping on Changing to a low-impact lifestyle can feel like a drag—the constant weighing-up of choices that you used to make without a thought can take its toll. When motivation's hard to come by, and you're feeling more inclined to throw in the towel than check whether it's made from organic cotton, it's time to give yourself a boost. If you've been keeping one, reach for your green journal (see pages 53–54) and **congratulate yourself on your planet-saving achievements (499)**.

Your eco-stamina will also improve if you give yourself something specific to aim for, so **set new green goals (500)** for you and your family. When you achieve your targets, **give the whole family a reward (501)**—perhaps a picnic, nature walk, or day at the beach.

502 Going, going, gone! If you need to raise money for a good cause, why not auction people's skills or some special experiences rather than physical items that may well end up as waste. For example: a romantic serenade, a week in someone's holiday home, lunch with someone famous, a harp lesson, a trip to your local TV studios, a luxury home-delivered organic breakfast. Use your imagination, and watch the bids go sky-high.

503 **Sticky labels** Put your children's wooden Popsicle sticks to good use by using them to label plants. Once the plants have grown large enough that they no longer need tags, you can bury the sticks in the soil, where they'll decompose to provide useful fiber.

504 **Spot-on spot treatment** Almost all of us experience acne at some point in our lives. While the uncannily bad timing of the eruptions may seem scary, the noxious concoctions we blithely dab on our perturbing pimples are a lot more frightening. Treatments based on organically grown essential oils (such as tea tree, which has antibacterial and anti-inflammatory properties) are much healthier for the environment, the people who cultivate them, and the people who use them.

505 **Recycled countertops** Next time you remodel your home or workplace, put some disposable packaging into long-term employment by specifying work surfaces, table tops, or doors to be made out of sheets of recycled plastic. The unique patterns created by melting yogurt pots, plastic cups, or even cellphones serve as a beautiful focal point, as well as durable surfaces that will last for years.

506 **A FAIR EXCHANGE**

Children usually grow out of clothes and other paraphernalia well before they're worn out. Instead of buying everything new, lend, borrow, and swap equipment with friends whose children are older or younger than yours. You can also pick up secondhand bargains in good condition from thrift shops and on auction or exchange websites (see page 372).

---

507 **Clean sweep** Use a broom instead of a hose to clean your driveway, patio, and paths. If necessary, use a quick sluice of water (ideally left over from doing the dishes) to wash away any remaining dust once you've finished sweeping.

508 **Focused organic shopping** World consumption of chemical pesticides and fertilizers is exploding—from 30 million tons a year in 1960 to 140 million four decades later—and this trend is unlikely to stop unless consumers demand it. If you can't get hold of a full range of organic groceries, or have a limited budget, prioritize buying organic items that are particularly laden with chemicals in conventional agriculture. Make an effort always to buy organic bread (and other wheat products), apples, celery, strawberries, peaches, grapes, spinach, and pears to avoid the worst chemical overloads.

509 **Travel light** Take nothing but pictures; leave nothing but footprints.

510 **Do it right** Want to make sure your do-it-yourself project will have minimal environmental impact? Ask the experts. Visit a specialist eco store (online or in person) to find out about the growing number of environmental building products and techniques available.

511 **One person's junk . . .** If you're having a clear-out, hold a garage sale or a tag sale. By decluttering in this way, you'll ensure that your unwanted items will go to people who have use for them, rather than just ending up at the dump.

512 **Don't kill with kindness** Feeding bread to ducks and other waterfowl is a popular way to spend time in the park, but it may do more harm than good. The bread makes the ducks feel full, but doesn't give them the nutrients they require, leaving them vulnerable to illness.

513 **Keep it sleek** Modern cars are designed to be aerodynamic, slipping through the air with minimum friction and maximum fuel efficiency. Luggage racks have exactly the opposite effect—so don't keep them on the car unless you're planning to use them, especially if you're going on a long, high-speed journey.

514 **Greener golfing** Golf is good for getting outdoors, but it's not always great for the environment. So try to reduce the ecological impact of your fun on the greens. A good start would be to **join an environmentally friendly golf club (515)**.

It should have features such as naturally weed-resistant grass to minimize pesticide use, and a watering system that uses reclaimed water. For the benefit of your health as well as the environment, **walk the course instead of using a golf cart (516)**. If you need to use a cart, keep to the designated paths to avoid straying onto natural habitats for wildlife, and urge your club to replace its fleet with electric-powered ones, if they haven't already. And while you're at it, **let your club know you'd rather play on brown grass (517)** during periods of low rainfall than on needlessly watered fairways. The grass will soon recover when it starts to rain again.

518 **Monitor your car's appetite** If your car starts doing fewer miles to the gallon than normal, its engine may need tuning. So calculate your miles per gallon each time you fill your tank (divide the number of miles traveled since the last fill-up by the number of gallons purchased this time). If your fuel economy drops significantly, and there's no other obvious explanation (such as an increase in stop-start urban driving), get your car checked out as soon as possible.

519 **Countertop baking** If you often bake small meals, consider investing in a toaster oven, which uses less than half as much energy as a conventional oven.

---

520 **FLY A KITE!** Get the whole family outdoors enjoying the power of the wind. You'll get fit, improve your coordination, and have fun. Buy a secondhand kite or make your own (see page 372).

---

521 **Shady behavior** If you have French doors opening onto a patio, fit them with awnings, so that in hot weather you can keep the sun out, reducing the need for air-conditioning. The awnings will also give you a pleasant shaded area to spend time on the patio.

522 Make the most of your fan Surprising as it may seem, it may be worth using your ceiling fan in the winter as well as the summer. By reversing the direction of the blades in the winter, you push warmer air down, causing heat to be distributed throughout the house, which means that your heating system doesn't have to work as hard.

523 Do you really need a fur coat? Traditionally seen as a sign of wealth, fur coats are a costly way to keep warm in more ways than one. Most real fur coats use pelts from fur farms, where animals are often kept in inhumane conditions. Unlike most "natural" products, real fur is also bad for the environment: it requires a huge amount of energy to produce and is processed with carcinogenic formaldehyde and chromium.

Fake fur is little better. Although involving no cruelty to animals, it is made from nylon, which is manufactured from oil—about a third of a barrel for the average coat—producing toxic nitrous oxide emissions along the way.

If you can't resist the allure of fur, the lowest-impact options are to **acquire a secondhand or vintage garment (524)**, or buy a new item made from recycled pelts.

525 Give leather shoes the boot Next time you need to buy some new footwear, look for alternatives to virgin leather. Around 95 percent of leather products are chrome-tanned, producing waste certified as "hazardous." Vegan shoes are made from a variety of non-leather materials, but bear in mind that if they're plastic-based they're likely to have a high environmental impact. Instead, **look for shoes made from recycled materials (526)**, which are just beginning to move from worthy to desirable. Look for shoes with soles made from recycled rubber (often from car tires) and uppers made of everything from leather rescued from old car seats to cotton from reclaimed jeans and surplus military jackets.

Whatever material they're made from, **get maximum mileage out of your shoes (527)** by looking after them properly. Invest in some shoe trees (ideally wooden) to help your shoes retain their shape, clean them regularly, particularly if they're leather (apart from making them look smarter, this will help keep the leather watertight), and have them resoled and reheeled whenever they begin to wear down.

528 **Runny nose?** Use a handkerchief, rather than paper tissues to blow your nose. Not only will this save trees, but the (ideally organic) cotton will be kinder to your nose than the wood fibers in tissues.

529 **Dip into a dumpster** House clearances and refurbishments generate lots of goodies destined for landfill that still have plenty of mileage in them. Look for building activity in your area—it could yield a sink, sofa, or sideboard perfect for your home. Be sure to ask before you take items if they're in someone's driveway. Their previous owners will usually be delighted you're lightening their load.

530 **Need a new carpet?** If you're planning to replace your carpet, look into recycled versions. Their hard-wearing surface is particularly good for high-traffic areas such as offices and hallways. And instead of lobbing it into landfill, **recycle your old carpet (531)**. There are companies that will take worn-out carpet away and process it into new carpet, as well as all kinds of other products—from parking barriers to car components.

532 **SEE THE FOREST FOR THE TREES** Mahogany and teak are beautiful, high-quality tropical hardwoods that take many decades to mature and often come from endangered forests. If you need a hardwood, look for an approved-source program, or try a responsible company that plants and sustainably harvests its own.

533 **PVC-exclusion zone** Polyvinyl chloride (PVC) is a source of hormone-disrupting chemicals and is potentially carcinogenic. Make sure it doesn't sneak into your home in wallpaper, shower curtains, water pipes, or other plastic components. Carefully read descriptions on packaging, and if you're having building work done, insist on using alternative materials.

534 **Strip your paint safely** Steer clear of solvent-based products. Besides giving you a nasty headache, burning your skin, and discoloring wood, they damage the environment at the time of manufacture and point of use. The high levels of volatile organic compounds (VOCs) they contain contribute to the depletion of the ozone layer and may be carcinogenic. To avoid these unpleasant side effects, use water-based paint-strippers. They're pH-neutral, biodegradable, and much more pleasant to use.

535 **Looking for unique wallpaper?** Try using sheets of unwanted music, pages from your favorite magazines, or spreads from the newspapers you most respect to create one-of-a-kind, striking décor. If you get tired of looking at any areas, simply paper over them in an ever-evolving montage.

536 **Stay sharp** Invest in a sharpening stone or other device to keep your kitchen knives razor sharp. Used regularly, this will keep good-quality knives in perfect form indefinitely. So there's no need to keep forking out for new blades to satisfy your carrot-chopping habit.

537 **Lumber liability** Be wary of lumber with a pale green stain: this is a sign that the wood has been pressure treated with the toxic compound chromated copper arsenate (CCA) to protect it against rot and pests. Although the sale of CCA-treated wood was banned in the U.S. at the end of 2003, most existing fencing, decking and wooden outdoor furniture will have been constructed from it. On no account burn CCA-treated lumber, as this will release arsenic into your immediate atmosphere. Instead, take it to your local recycling center for safer disposal.

538 **Breath of fresh air** Try to watch a few hours' less TV each week, and spend the time you gain enjoying being outdoors engaged in carbon-neutral leisure activities—out with friends or family, pottering around in the garden, or simply sitting in the shade of a tree with your nose buried in a good book.

539 **Festive sparkle** Making trimmings for Christmas and other special occasions—particularly with children to help—is so much fun that once you've tried it, you'll never buy another decoration again. For example, you can **make tree decorations from a stiff dough (540)** of flour, water, and a little salt. Use cookie cutters to form the shape (or design your own), then bake them in a hot oven until they're hard. Remember to make a little hole in the top to loop string or ribbon through. Adorn your decorations with paints, seeds, glitter, or feathers. Packed away carefully after Christmas, these treasures should last decades. Shapes cut from felt also make great hanging decorations, and you can **fashion magnificent paper chains (541)** from colorful magazines and old wrapping paper.

Deck your home in a drift of dancing snowflakes (542) by cutting out circular pieces of (recycled) white paper, then folding each one in half three times and cutting v-shaped nicks into the edges of the triangle you've made. Unfold it and feed a loop of thread through one of the perforations. Depending on their size, you can use these flakes to decorate your tree or hang them from the ceiling, where they'll dance in the breeze. Like the real thing, every one you make will be unique.

543 **Virtual faxing** Use your computer to send and receive faxes, rather than sending hard copies. That way the recipient can decide whether they really need to print out your message or just read it on their screen.

544 **Rerelease an album** Impress a music-loving friend by giving them a decorative bowl made from a recycled vinyl record. Vinyl is the second most commonly produced plastic in the world and desperately needs a retirement home.

545 **Trash mob** Give some "tender, loving care" to a trash-strewn green space in your neighborhood by organizing a litter blitz with some friends or neighbors. Divide the litter into recyclable categories and discard the rest. Then take off your gloves, wash your hands, and have a picnic in your newly reclaimed green area (don't forget to pick up your wrappers!).

546 **Switch off while you soap up** It's all too easy to lose track of time when you're in the shower (whether or not you're singing). To save water, turn off the shower once you're wet, lather up with soap and shampoo at your leisure, and turn the flow back on only once you're ready to rinse off.

547 **Idling time** Turn off your engine if you're going to be stationary for more than two minutes. You'll save fuel and avoid unnecessary wear to cylinders, spark plugs and the exhaust system.

548 **Happy wrapper** Look for unbleached parchment paper for kitchen use. This has none of the chemical compounds often to be found in bleached parchment paper. After use, you can scrunch it up to provide valuable fiber for your compost pile.

If you do a lot of baking, cut down on your parchment-paper use by **buying a reusable silicone baking sheet (549)**.

550 **A period of consequences** In 1936, just before the Second World War, Sir Winston Churchill said: "The era of procrastination, of half-measures, of soothing and baffling expedients, of delays, is coming to its close. In its place we are entering a period of consequences." Insurance companies are now refusing to provide cover for buildings in some low-lying regions, as the risk of flooding resulting from extreme climate patterns has become so great. Previously unaffected cities around the globe are threatened by the invasion of malaria-carrying mosquitoes as the high altitudes they were built at to avoid just this problem become warmer. This could be a battle we'll need to fight on a number of fronts, and as we learn more about the impacts of our way of life on the world around us, we'll need to find ways of changing the direction we're headed in.

551 MICRO-GARDENING You don't need a garden to develop a green thumb—you can grow herbs on your kitchen windowsill, lettuce and other salad greens in window boxes, and potatoes in a stack of old tires filled with soil mix (see page 114).

552 **Wear the right jeans for the job** If you're working hard on a home-improvement or gardening challenge, get yourself some super-durable hemp jeans. Hemp fiber is about three times stronger than cotton, as well as having unimpeachable environmental credentials (see page 109).

553 **Shop at the dump** Before you go on a spending spree at the home center or furniture shop, see what bargains are available at your local dump or recycling center. Some sell items such as lumber and furniture for small change. Perfect material for do-it-yourself projects.

554 **Inspiration and aspiration** Environmentally responsible design and architecture used to suffer from an unattractive image. But all that's changing as a new generation of designers and building contractors take on the challenge of making gorgeously eco-friendly places that even the most aesthetically discerning among us would aspire to live in. Marvel at the inspirational creations highlighted in eco-building features on home and garden television shows.

555 **Make a butterfly box** Many beautiful varieties of butterfly are under threat as human activity encroaches upon their habitats. You can help to reverse this trend. Cut large windows in the sides of a lidded cardboard box, and cover them with fine black netting. Collect plants or weeds, such as nettles, that have caterpillars on them. Put the stalks in a jam jar of water, place in the box, and provide new plants as the old ones are eaten by the caterpillars. Protected from birds, the caterpillars will turn into pupae and emerge as butterflies to be released into the wild.

556 **Ask not to be embalmed** Now that we have refrigerated mortuaries, there's no need for embalming fluids to preserve bodies before burial or cremation. So make sure your relatives know you'd rather skip this toxin-heavy process.

557 **Give your windows a treat** Draperies and other window treatments can make a real difference to the way a room looks, as well as keeping your home cozy in winter and blocking out unwanted heat in summer. Since they're subjected to limited wear and tear, quality secondhand draperies are often an excellent buy—check out your local thrift shop.

558 **Pets don't need TV dinners!** Avoid single-serving pouches of dog and cat food. These imitations of human prepackaged meals are a waste of money and packaging. Buy your petfood in bulk, and save these dainty sachets for very occasional pet meals away from home, if you buy them at all.

559 **Don't pick on small fry** When you're choosing fish, avoid buying undersize or immature ones. The younger they are, the less likely they are to have had a chance to breed before being caught, so the greater the impact of your meal on the depletion of fish stocks.

560 **How can we improve your stay?** If you're staying at a hotel, motel, or bed-and-breakfast that doesn't seem to have paid much attention to saving energy and resources, give the management some ideas about how they could pep up their environmental performance (see page 373).

561 **Pass on unwanted footwear** Charities are always grateful to accept lightly worn shoes that you've grown out of or gotten bored with for sale in their shops or for delivery to needy recipients. So clear out that dusty shoe graveyard under your bed, and send your unloved footwear packing.

562 **Take them to the cleaners** If you've got a dry cleaning or professional laundry habit, you've also probably got a huge colony of wire coathangers breeding in your closet. Why not take them back to the cleaners with your next load of laundry for them to reuse?

563 **Liberate yourself from the laundry** Despite what detergent ads might lead us to believe, most clothes don't need washing after every wearing. That's not to say that you should wait until they can walk to the washing machine by themselves, but don't launder them before they're actually dirty.

There are several tricks you can use to keep clothes fresh. For example, **put away "clean enough" clothes right after wearing (564)** to stop them from mixing with the truly unwearable stuff. If they're only slightly crumpled or stale,

hang already-worn garments outside or by a window to air (565), or in the bathroom while you take a shower to steam out light creases.

Apart from benefiting the environment, washing and drying clothes less often keeps them looking newer for longer. And with less laundry to do, you'll have more time and money for the activities you actually enjoy.

---

566 **TURN YOUR SHOES INTO A FOOTBALL FIELD**

When your shoes are beyond resuscitation by even the most skilled cobbler, make sure they're recycled rather than sent to landfill. The rubber in their soles has a multitude of uses—for example, as an ingredient of the "turf" for all-weather sports fields.

---

567 **Look for the blue check mark** Take the guesswork out of ethical fish-buying by looking for fish products carrying a symbol that incorporates a blue check mark into the outline of a fish. This shows that the fish has been certified as coming from a sustainable source by the Marine Stewardship Council (MSC).

568 **Fruitful activity** Get your children involved in cultivating some fruit and vegetables from scratch. Grow strawberries in pots, plant a few blueberry bushes, or sow a couple of rows of carrot seeds. If you haven't got space to grow your own, **go on an outing to a "pick-your-own" fruit farm (569)**.

570 **Water funnel** Use an upturned plastic bottle with the bottom chopped off and the neck buried in the ground to channel water directly to plants' and trees' roots, where it's really needed. Otherwise, during dry spells, any water's likely to run off the surface of the soil so that little gets to your plants.

571 **Take yourself off the menu** Keep biting insects at bay with organic, chemical-free, herbal-based repellents. Most conventional insect repellents contain a pesticide called DEET, which can have many nasty side effects—ranging from rashes to convulsions—and is bad for the environment. Natural options are readily available, work just as well, and smell better.

572 **Cistern alert** Put a few drops of food coloring into your toilet cistern. If it seeps into the bowl, you know that you have a leak. Fixing it will be easy, and can save more than 250 gallons of water a month.

573 **Caviar caveat** It may not cross your path often, but when it does, turn your nose up at beluga caviar. The market in sturgeon eggs has reduced the number of these fish in the Caspian Sea by 90 percent in the last 30 years, and the entire population is under such threat that some countries have now banned imports of beluga in an attempt to save the species. You'll be pleased to know there are sustainable options—**look for onuga "caviar" (574)** from the more plentiful herring. And wash it down with some biodynamic champagne (see pages 202–203)!

575 **Don't stick with nonstick** Use stainless steel saucepans or iron-bottom cookware instead of nonstick pans. Overheated nonstick surfaces release fumes that kill birds such as canaries very quickly—which doesn't bode well for the inhabitants (feathered or otherwise) of your kitchen.

576 **Junk faxes** Stop your home or work fax machine from churning through paper unnecessarily (and annoying you incessantly) by barring unsolicited faxes. Contact a mail/fax preference service (see page 371) to have your fax number made unavailable to unsolicited callers.

577 **Rake's progress** Rake up dead leaves instead of using a leaf blower—you'll save energy, get strong arms, and avoid annoying the neighbors. If you really need a power tool for a hard-to-reach spot like the roof, **use an electric leaf blower rather than a gasoline-powered one (578)**. They're usually quieter and more energy efficient. However you gather your leaves, make them into leaf mold (see pages 250–251) to feed your garden, rather than just throwing them away.

579 RELEASE YOUR BOOKS INTO THE WILD Once you've read a book, leave it on a bench, or in some other public place, with a note inviting whoever finds it to take it, read it, then rerelease it. If you write in an ID number, available by registering online (see page 371), you can track your book as it changes hands, and consider how many trees have been saved.

580 **Pens and pencils** Stock up on pens and markers that contain nontoxic ink, and crayons made from soybean oil instead of more harmful chemicals. And **look for pens and pencils made from recycled materials (581)**. Many attractive and effective writing implements are now made from plastic, newspapers, fabrics, and even money. For maximum effect, ask your employer to supply them in your workplace.

582 **Stop wasting wine without getting wasted** Much as you might like to use the "waste not, want not" principle as a pretext for overindulgence, you don't have to finish a bottle of wine in one sitting to stop leftover wine from going sour. The key to keeping wine for another occasion is to stop it from becoming exposed to oxygen. Using an inexpensive vacuum pump to remove the air from the bottle and stoppering it with a reusable rubber "cork," the wine will keep fresh for several days. You'll cut back on hangovers and create fewer empty bottles to recycle.

583 **Eco-friendly tippling** Biodynamic wine is the product of a holistic process of organic agriculture that works with the rhythms of nature. Planting and harvesting take place with an eye to the phases of the moon, and the soil is viewed not simply as a growth medium for the grapes but as an organism in its own right. While this ethos may sound far out, biodynamic wine has the very real benefit of being free from harmful fumigants, insecticides, fungicides, and herbicides. Studies show that biodynamic farms have more organic matter and microbial activity in their soil than conventional counterparts. And anecdotal evidence suggests that biodynamic wine drinkers are among the Earth's happiest creatures!

584 **Grass-free gardening** If you're looking for a way to cut down on the amount of mowing and watering your garden needs, you could try replacing your lawn with some alternative ground cover, such as yarrow, thyme, alyssum, sweet woodruff, or periwinkle. Ask a local nursery which plants would best tolerate your local growing conditions.

585 **Concentrate!** Try to buy concentrated products (such as dishwashing liquid) whenever possible. That way you won't be paying extra for products heavy with water that you can easily add yourself.

586 **Make some feathered friends** Nesting sites can be at a premium, particularly in urban areas. Put up some bird houses around your garden and watch (from a discreet distance) the residents' families grow in their secure new homes. Remember to **clean out your bird houses (587)** at the end of each breeding season to reduce the risk of spreading parasites or infection.

Having sheltered them, make sure that you also **feed the birds in your garden (588)**—particularly through the winter. Stock up your supplies regularly and reliably with a range of suitable foods (see page 370). For a special treat, **make a fat ball (589)**: melt some suet or lard (vegetable oils aren't suitable) and stir in nuts, seeds, and raisins, pour the mixture into a small bowl and part-submerge a piece of string in it. Put the bowl in the fridge to solidify, then remove the ball and tie it to a branch with the string.

590 **Leave your lawnmowings on the lawn** Instead of throwing them away and then covering your hallowed turf with fertilizers, let grass clippings rot into the lawn, where they'll release nutrients back into the soil. Just make sure you mow when the grass is dry, so that the cuttings don't clump, which can stifle new growth.

591 **Make your fish go further** If you want to keep fish in your diet, choose carefully, and make sure you don't waste a single bit of these precious creatures. Use the heads and bones to make stock for fish stews or soups, and give the skins to a grateful pet cat or dog.

592 **NOBLE ROT** Rotting wood is a common feature of wild ecosystems. It recycles nutrients back into the soil and provides a habitat for a wide range of creatures—as you'll know if you've ever peered underneath a decaying log. So help things along by leaving a few logs to rot in an unobtrusive part of your garden.

593 **Outflank garden pests** You can now buy batches of natural predators such as ladybugs, predatory mites, and lacewings through gardening sites on the internet. These handy creatures can help keep pests at bay without the need for chemical treatments. But be sure to check that they'll eat only the critters you want to get rid of, or you could upset the natural balance of your garden.

594 **Horticultural pick-me-up** To boost your garden's fertility, try adding bonemeal, wood ash, or spiral stone meal to your compost. These natural substances won't leach nitrates into groundwater, so you'll avoid contributing to the distortion of aquatic ecosystems by synthetic fertilizers.

595 **Hoedown** To ensure that your plants benefit fully from any water you give them, take a moment to lightly hoe the soil around them first. This breaks up any crust that may have formed on the surface of the flower bed, allowing water to penetrate the surface and sink down to the roots, where it's really needed.

596 **Salad savvy** If you're making a salad with hard-boiled eggs, keep the cold water from rinsing the salad leaves to plunge the cooked eggs into to cool them down—and don't forget to keep the nutrient-rich water that you boiled the eggs in for feeding your houseplants or the garden (see page 60)!

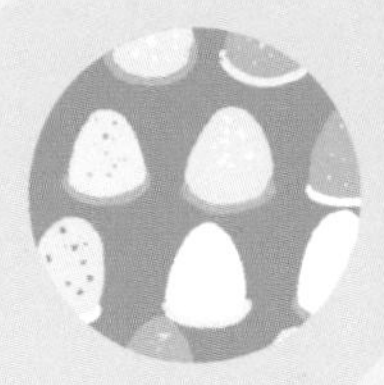

597 **Try dye** Look for clothing and other items colored with subtly beautiful natural dyes. And if you're feeling adventurous, you could even try making your own pigments from roots, nuts, bark, or flowers. Choose blossoms that are in full bloom, ripe berries, and mature nuts, and remember never to gather more than half the crop of anything growing in the wild, so that the plant can regenerate. To make the dye solution, chop the plant material into small pieces and place it in a pot. Cover with double the amount of water, bring to the boil, then simmer for about an hour. Strain, then add the fabric to be dyed. For a stronger shade, leave it to soak overnight. Depending on the dye, you may need to presoak the fabric in a mordant (fixative) to ensure that the color sets.

598 **Ice your wine** Instead of pouring away leftover wine, drain undrunk glasses into ice cube containers and store in the freezer for the next time you need wine to cook with. No lingering germs will survive the freezing and boiling processes, and you won't need to crack open a fresh bottle for the pot.

599 **Bag your bags** If you buy packaged food, rinse the plastic wrap or bag it came in for reuse. Many types of plastic can be used again and again, so you should never need to buy sandwich bags or plastic wrap to cover your food.

600 **A good old soak** To save water (and elbow grease), leave pots and pans with stubborn food remains on them to soak for a while before you try to wash them, rather than holding them under running water while you scrape them clean.

601 **Watch and learn** Watch nature documentaries with your children and vicariously enjoy the wonders of the natural world. *National Geographic* and the British Broadcasting Corporation have produced some magnificent programs, which should inspire even the most Playstation-obsessed youngsters to care for their planet.

602 **Lesser of two evils** It's healthiest for your garden to keep it completely free from chemicals. But if you have an exceptional reason to use a chemical treatment—perhaps you've suffered an infestation of a particularly vigorous weed—try to find the most benign one available. Check that it's specifically designed for garden use, and apply it in the smallest quantity possible in only the precise area needed. Try to find a product designed to address your particular problem, rather than a broad-spectrum toxin such as atrazine or lindane, which will indiscriminately kill any living organism it touches.

603 **Moth watch** Moths are often considered just butterflies' dowdy relatives. But they have a subtle beauty of their own, which you can really appreciate during a nocturnal moth-spotting session. Attract the moths with an outdoor light, and hang an old white sheet or cloth beneath it for them to land on. Get up close to observe their beautiful, muted markings and colors. If you have children, let them join in—apart from anything else, they'll enjoy staying up late!

604 **The boy on the beach** Ponder the story of a little boy on a beach throwing stranded starfish back into the ocean. "Why do you bother?" a man asked him. "There are hundreds of them. You couldn't possibly save them all." "No," the little boy answered, "but I can save this one, and it makes a difference to him."

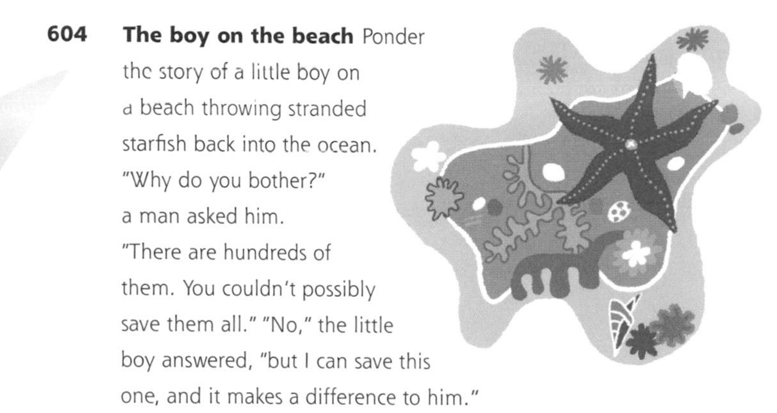

605 **Cooler rinse** A washing machine uses up to 90 percent of its energy heating water. A warm wash and cold rinse will work just as well on nearly all clothes as a hot wash and warm rinse.

606 **Scald your weeds** Instead of using environmentally damaging herbicides or fungicides to keep weeds at bay, try pouring boiling water on them. The plants will shrivel and die, leaving no toxic residues. Just remember to boil only as much water as you need, and be careful not to pour it on your legs!

607 **Cool school uniform** If your children wear a uniform to school, chances are it'll be made from artificial fibers that leave your kids hot and sticky and have unpleasant environmental impacts. Look for Fairtrade, organic-cotton school clothing, and **give details of green suppliers to your children's school (608)**.

Children often grow out of their uniform well before it's worn out. So whether or not you manage to find ethically sourced fabrics, **pass on outgrown uniform to younger siblings or other pupils (609)**. And, if it hasn't already done so, **ask your school to set up a secondhand uniform shop (610)**—it's likely that many other parents would be keen to take advantage of such a money-saving idea.

611 **As if you'd never been there** Camping is a low-impact way to see the world if you take a little care. **Select a site that's already been used (612)**, to avoid encroaching on virgin ground. Be extremely vigilant when making campfires (if allowed), and **always dampen your fireplace afterward (613)** to make sure it's fully extinguished. Leave as little trace of your presence as possible: **take all your trash away with you (614)**. Wash yourself, your dishes, and your clothes at least 100 feet

away from rivers, streams, lakes, or ponds to **avoid polluting water sources (615)**. Use biodegradable soaps, and pour washing water onto the ground rather than into streams. That goes for brushing your teeth, too.

616 **Don't con your air con** Make sure that your air conditioning system's getting the right message about the temperature of your home. Placing a heat-generating appliance such as a lamp or TV near the thermostat will fool it into overdrive, making it blast out more cool air than necessary. And if you think that's cold, your next electricity bill will really send a shiver down your spine.

617 **A hedge can be a home** If you've got a dilapidated garden fence that needs replacing, consider planting a hedge instead. You won't need to coat it in potentially harmful wood preservative, and it will provide food, shelter, and maternity facilities for many kinds of wildlife, including birds and butterflies. To give indigenous creatures a home they can relate to, **choose a species of plant native to your region (618)**. When it has become established (or if you've already got a mature hedge), go easy with the trimming shears. **Leave pruning back until winter is well and truly over (619)**, so that the hedge provides shelter throughout the coldest months. **Don't trim it again until late summer (620)**, to avoid disturbing nesting birds, and **leave berries to develop (621)** so that there'll be a source of food over winter.

622 **Nurture some nettles** If you have space, let a patch of nettles grow in your garden. They attract butterflies, bind the soil, and provide it with a rich source of nutrients. Simply cut them at the base at the end of the summer and leave them to rot into the ground, or add them to your compost pile. While they're still young and tender, you can **harvest nettles to make tea, steam as a delicious vegetable, or blend into soups (623)**. Just remember to wear thick gloves when picking them!

624 **Set up a wormery** If you have limited space for composting, a wormery could be the solution. These compact compost containers house brandling worms, which eat up to half their own weight in waste every day. You can buy a full kit, complete with worms, or get the worms separately from a fishing or composting supplier. The worms eat virtually any organic kitchen waste, including peelings, cooked and uncooked scraps, and teabags. You'll end up with a top-quality compost, as well as a fertilizing liquid which can be collected from a tap at the bottom of the wormery, diluted 1:10 with water, and used as an all-purpose plant feed. However, **don't put citrus peel, onions, or garlic in the wormery (625)**—the worms don't like them.

626 Harness the heat from beneath your feet You may think of soil as cold and damp, but in fact a few feet below the surface, the ground is warm all year round. This natural heat can be transferred by a geothermal heat pump to warm your home. In this beautifully simple system, fluid flows through a network of pipes buried in the ground, where it absorbs the natural warmth. Once warmed, the liquid is pumped up to a heat condensor where it "gives up" its heat to your central heating system. In the summer the system can be reversed to cool your home. Such systems are becoming de rigueur for any self-respecting new eco-development and can also be retrofitted into an existing home. They may not be cheap to install, but will save you a lot in heating bills. Satisfied customers include Elton John and the queen of England.

627 Snow limits If you want to ski or snowboard off the beaten track, ask your local ski guide for advice about where to go. In some areas, going off-trail can cause severe damage to the natural environment and even increase the risk of avalanches. Always stay within the boundaries of the ski resort, especially where it borders on a national park or conservation area.

628 **TURN IT DOWN** Many homes are much warmer than necessary in the winter. Try turning the heating down a touch. You're unlikely to notice the difference in temperature, but every degree Fahrenheit you reduce it by should save nearly 5 percent on your heating bill. If you're feeling chilly, **put a sweater on, or do some chores (629)** before you turn up the heat. You'll probably find you're more than warm enough.

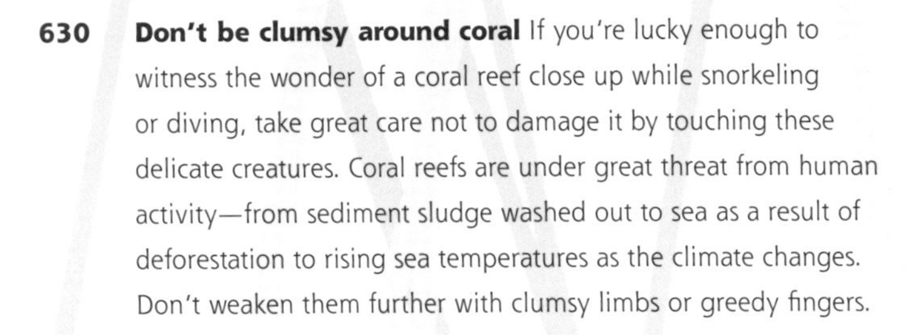

630 **Don't be clumsy around coral** If you're lucky enough to witness the wonder of a coral reef close up while snorkeling or diving, take great care not to damage it by touching these delicate creatures. Coral reefs are under great threat from human activity—from sediment sludge washed out to sea as a result of deforestation to rising sea temperatures as the climate changes. Don't weaken them further with clumsy limbs or greedy fingers.

631 **Hands off!** Wildflowers look so pretty growing in their natural setting, it can be tempting to try taking some of that beauty home. But wild species tend not to last long when picked, so leave them to flourish in their natural habitat. If you'd like to enjoy some wild floral beauty at home, **sow some open-pollinated "heritage" seeds in your garden (632)**.

633 **Way to go, Kyoto!** Averting global warming and climate change (see page 17) requires concerted action from individuals, organizations, and nations worldwide. The Kyoto Protocol (effective from 2005), an international treaty requiring signatories to limit their emissions of greenhouse gases, is a good start. It will limit emissions by only a small fraction of what's needed to get

back to steady atmospheric and climatic levels, and a few nations are yet to sign up. But it's setting a precedent for more stringent initiatives, and inspiring action even within countries that haven't ratified the treaty—such as the U.S., where more than 300 mayors have pledged that their cities will meet the Kyoto targets.

Find out what your government, region, or city is doing to limit CO_2 emissions (634), and pledge your support for bigger reductions.

635 **Burnished gold** Clean gold jewelry gently with toothpaste, or a paste of salt, vinegar, and flour. Try using an old toothbrush to access all the surfaces of intricate designs.

636 **Green home away from home** Needing to look after its guests' every need around the clock, the average hotel guzzles a huge amount of energy. The good news is that more and more hotels are becoming environmentally friendly as interest in green issues grows, and more will convert if there's sufficient demand. Show your support by choosing somewhere to stay from a directory of "green" hotels (see page 373).

637 **Pamper your worms** Calcified seaweed is a useful addition to a wormery (see page 215), helping to neutralize the acid content of foods you put in. However, there's concern that overharvesting is threatening some seaweed beds. A good alternative is crushed eggshells. Try baking the shells in the residual heat of the oven after cooking to make them easier to crush into little pieces.

638 **Make a splash** Play in, on, and under the water with barely a ripple of ecological impact in a canoe, kayak, raft, sailing boat, windsurfboard, or row boat, or try snorkeling, swimming, or diving. You'll get into real contact with the aquatic environment in a way that's impossible if you're attacking it on emission-spewing jet skis or a motorboat, you'll get some decent exercise, and other people on the beach will be thankful for the peace!

639 **From hair dryer to air dryer** Allowing your hair to dry naturally not only saves you time and money but is much better for your hair, which is likely to become brittle if subjected to a daily blast of scalp-tinglingly hot air. So save your energy-guzzling hair dryer for occasions when you need an extra-special coiffure or it's simply too cold to go outside with even remotely wet hair.

640 **Skimp on shrimp** Approximately 55 billion pounds of fish, sharks, and seabirds die each year as "bycatch"—creatures caught accidentally as a result of indiscriminate fishing techniques. Because it uses particularly fine-mesh nets, shrimp fishing is one of the worst culprits. For every thousand of us who stop eating shrimp, we can save more than 11,000 pounds of sea life per year. Alternatively, try to **encourage demand for some of the tasty but neglected species in the bycatch (641)**, such as gurnard and witch flounder. Ask your local fish dealer to stock these plentiful fish and try out some new recipes with them.

---

642 **CHOOSE UGLY VEGGIES** Odd shapes and unusual pigments generally have no impact on the flavor of produce, but by insisting on strict uniformity, supermarkets force farmers to waste huge amounts of food, and limit the variety sold. This also cuts the farmers' profit margins, driving them to more intensive methods. Let retailers know you'd be delighted to eat varied veggies and funny fruit, and enjoy the diversity in shape, color, and size that nature intended.

643 **Let's look after our fish** Thanks to our insatiable appetite for fish, more than half of the species caught commercially are being fished so aggressively they can't breed fast enough to keep up, and some stocks are severely threatened. You can help to protect endangered fish by choosing to **buy species that aren't threatened (644)**, such as trout and bass. Bear in mind also that a species that's in plentiful supply in one fishery may be endangered in another. Consult a sustainable-seafood website (see page 372) for the latest details. **If you're ordering or buying fish, ask your waiter or fish dealer where it was caught (645)**, and, if they don't know, move your business to a more knowledgeable supplier.

If you eat fish for health reasons, you could **consider switching to other foods that contain the same nutrients (646)**. For example, flaxseed oil, rapeseed oil, and walnuts are good alternative sources of the omega-3 fatty acids to be found in oily fish such as salmon, tuna, and mackerel—try preparing yourself a delicious salad topped with chopped walnuts and finished with a flaxseed-oil dressing.

647 **A barrel of laughs** Beer drinkers can save the planet, too. Make your trips to the bar less wasteful by drinking draft beer, rather than beer in bottles. To minimize beer transportation costs, choose local brews if possible, or, better still, seek out bars that brew their own beer.

Similarly, when you're organizing a large party, **order beer in kegs or barrels (648)** rather than bottles or cans, and return them to the brewery afterward. It'll work out much cheaper, and your friends will enjoy the novelty of free beer on tap.

649 **Seal your ducts** A forced-air heating or cooling system uses ducts to circulate hot or cold air evenly around your home. Leaky ducts can reduce energy efficiency by around 10 percent. Apart from higher-than-normal utility bills, signs that your ducts are leaking include low air flow from certain registers or streaks of dust at registers or duct connections. If you suspect a problem, get your system checked out by a specialist contractor.

650 **"Green" tea** Even the humble cup of tea can be made more eco-friendly. Your first step should be to buy organic, Fairtrade tea. Check that the tea bags are made from recycled, unbleached paper. The next suggestion may have some people turning up their noses, but try it—it works! **Use each tea bag twice (651)**. Unless you're a fan of extremely strong tea, this will allow you to get two cups for the price of one. If you're making tea for more than one person, **use a teapot (652)**—you'll need fewer tea bags than if you put one in each mug.

Of course, there's no need for tea bags at all. Why not **opt for loose-leaf tea instead (653)**? You'll save on paper, processing, and financial costs—and there's no more civilized way to enjoy a cup of tea. Whichever method of infusion you go for, remember to **compost your tea leaves (654)**. They're a great source of nutrients, and loose leaves can be spread directly onto the soil around the base of plants if you haven't got a compost pile.

655 **Interactive vacations** It's all too easy to travel the world in search of new experiences, only to end up sealed in a high ecological-impact tourist bubble with little real engagement with the place you're visiting or the people who live there.

If you're planning a vacation, why not look into the ever-expanding range of community-based tourism projects, which bring tourists into contact with local people. Accommodation ranges from roughing it to luxury lodges, and activities include learning to drum or speak a language, snorkeling, kayaking, and horse riding—as well as relaxing!

656 **A biodegradable stickup** Secure giftwrap with tape made from cellulose. The chlorine-free woodpulp it's made from is better for the environment than PVC or acetate alternatives (although it will pull paint off walls in exactly the same way as the toxic stuff, so don't use it to stick up posters!).

657 **Go on a naturally helpful vacation** If you want to do something constructive with your free time, try volunteering for one of the many conservation projects organized by specialist charities around the world. Organizations such as Earthwatch allow you to work alongside scientists on environmental projects worldwide, so you can interact directly with nature and learn about how best to look after animal and plant life.

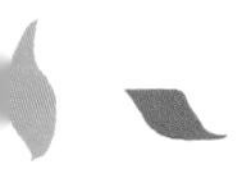

658 **Fill the page** Unless your document needs beautiful formatting for a picky reader, use a smaller-than-normal font size, single or 1.5 line spacing (rather than double), and narrow page margins to minimize the number of pages you need to print out.

659 **Filter out wasted paper** Rather than using bleached paper coffee filters, which may contain dioxins and are a very short-lived use of valuable trees, replace the filter in your coffee machine at home or work with a metal-mesh version, which can be reused thousands of times.

660 **Home infusions** Try growing your own herbal tea. Even the smallest windowsill can support a potted mint or chamomile plant. Simply pick a sprig every time you want a drink, rinse it, and leave to stand in a cup of freshly boiled water for five minutes. Delicious!

661 **Make your own notepad** Instead of using a brand new notebook for taking messages, keep a neat stack of scrap paper cut into quarters (stapled together into a pad if you prefer) next to the phone.

662 **HELP PROTECT THREATENED SPECIES** While the plight of charismatic large creatures such as whales, tigers, and pandas has attracted widespread attention, every day between fifty and a hundred lesser-known species of plant, animal, and insect become extinct. Help to protect countless unheralded species by restoring natural habitats in your local area and supporting international conservation efforts.

663 **Don't be a greedy angler** If you enjoy fishing, make sure your sport doesn't make too big a dent in fish stocks. **Catch only as much fish as you're going to eat (664)** or, depending on local regulations, catch and release fish—using a barbless hook, to minimize suffering and maximize the chances of survival of the fish you release. If you're fishing somewhere new, consult the local angling association or port authority to **familiarize yourself with local restrictions (665)** on where, when, and how you can fish and which species you're allowed to catch.

666 **Unpack your fridge** Make sure it's just you that's chilling out on vacation by emptying your fridge before you go away. Eat up leftovers, and give your neighbors any perishables you can't finish, rather than throwing them away. If there are things that will last and that you want to keep fresh, turn the power down to chill these few items. Otherwise turn the fridge off completely.

667 **Rules of the game** Contact with the environment is an integral part of many sports. But how much impact is your enjoyment having on the ecosystem it depends on? Is your baseball bat made from sustainable timber? Have any of your yachting friends ever emptied an oil tank on the water? Do mountaineers really leave only footprints on the summits they conquer? Find out whether there's an environmental charter for your sport. If there is, stick to it and urge other participants to do the same. If there isn't, contact your national sporting federation and encourage them to draw up and publicize a code of responsible behavior.

668 **When in Rome . . .** If you're traveling in far-flung places, be sure to sample the local gastronomic specialities. Locally produced food will be fresher and tastier than anything imported and will have caused much less pollution to get to your plate. You've got the rest of your life to eat what you normally have at home.

669 **Put your vacation in responsible hands** If you want to make sure that your vacation has a positive impact on the places you visit, choose a tour operator that has "responsible travel" policy. Such companies should offer a better exchange of culture with local people, demonstrably benefit conservation, and guarantee that some of the money you're paying for your vacation goes to local communities. Some operators donate to a local charity, or fund conservation and community projects in the destination.

670 **Kitchen storage solutions** Numerous foods come in jars and other containers that can be used over and over again. Large jars with screw lids are ideal for storing pantry basics such as pasta, rice, and legumes. Smaller containers are perfect for portions of salad, coleslaw, or other treats in lunchboxes. Not surprisingly, ice cream containers are great for holding portions of food to store in the freezer.

671 **Celebrate!** The world's not such a bad place, despite some of the challenges it may be facing. Don't forget to celebrate the joy of life here and now along the way—in the words of the baseball player Satchel Paige, "Work like you don't need the money, love like you've never been hurt, dance like nobody's watching."

672 **House hunting?** If you're buying a new home, look for one with good environmental credentials. Many countries now run accreditation programs for newly built houses, such as the LEED Green Building Rating System® in the United States and the BRE EcoHomes standard in Britain. Choosing a home with a favorable rating gives you a good head start in reducing your household's impact on the planet.

673 **Location, location, location** If you move, try to find a new home that's close to where you work, shop, and play. Being able to meet all your daily needs on foot is a great way to reduce your energy usage and associated emissions, helps you stay fit, and makes for great quality of life.

674 **Phosphate worse than death** Many laundry detergents contain phosphates, which soften hard water. Once they've done their job in your washing machine and gone through the sewage works, they can cause problems in waterways. Because algae feed on phosphates, high levels can cause algal blooms, which use up all the oxygen in the water, suffocating plant and animal life. Help to protect rivers and other waterways by choosing phosphate-free detergents and cleaning products.

675 **Don't keep taking the tablets** Instead of individual tablets of dishwasher or laundry detergent, choose boxes of loose powder or bottles of concentrated liquid to reduce packaging. Many health food stores offer bulk bins of detergent; bring your own container.

676 **A system that works on paper** Put a box next to each printer in your office for collecting paper that's been used only on one side. Keep it in a neat pile to reduce paper jams. Encourage your colleagues to use this supply for internal and informal documents.

677 **If in doubt, check it out** If you're not sure whether an item can be recycled, don't just toss it in the recycling bin anyway and hope for the best. Non-recyclables in the mix create extra work for recycling centers and can, in some cases, irredeemably contaminate whole batches of potentially reusable waste. Contact your local authority for guidance, and if they don't deal with the material in question, find out whether another organization does. If the item's totally non-recyclable, try not to buy it again in the future.

678 **Volunteer yourself some time off work** Many organizations allow—or actively encourage—employees to take time off to do voluntary work in the local community. If your employer doesn't run such a program, ask whether one can be set up, pointing out the good it would do for the company's public image. Besides deriving satisfaction from giving their time and skills to voluntary bodies, most people find that they learn a lot in the process.

---

679 **COMPLETE SHUTDOWN** Many modern TVs and computer monitors need to be unplugged in order fully to disable their standby setting. Incorporate this into your daily shutdown routine, and try to keep cables as untangled as possible so that you can easily identify which outlet to aim for.

680 **All your own work** Try making a food that you normally buy ready made—enjoy the satisfaction of sharing homemade pâté, bread, or cake with your surprised and impressed guests. Ask them all to bring something they've never made before to a party or picnic.

681 **Lead the way** Talk to your children about how your family can reduce its environmental impact. If they've grown up with the idea of conservation as a part of everyday life, they're more likely to want to get involved in (or at least accept) day-to-day activities such as turning off lights and appliances, driving less, and shopping for modestly packaged, recycled items.

682 **Carpet makeover** Just because your carpet's a little shabby or stained or no longer suits your interior décor, there's no need to replace it. Use a restoration service to re-dye or restore your carpet and avoid the far greater expense of buying and fitting a new one.

Similarly, if your carpet has annoying, unsightly puckers and wrinkles, don't head for the showroom just yet. Instead, **ask an accredited fitter to restretch it (683)**.

684 **Pedal your wares** Send deliveries around town quickly and cleanly using a bicycle courier service. Completely carbon neutral, despatch riders can nip among jammed traffic, which makes them the swiftest option for urban businesses, as well as helping to improve air quality.

685 **Clear winner** If you have the option, always choose products that come in glass rather than plastic containers. Glass is far less resource-hungry to produce and easier to reuse and recycle than plastic.

686 **Look up phone numbers online** Do you really need a new phone directory each year? If you look up numbers only occasionally, ask your phone company not to deliver a phone book and look up numbers online or over the phone instead. You'll save paper and shelf space, and be guaranteed to get the most up-to-date information.

687 **Artificial fibers are the pits** The body odor caused by clothes made from nylon and polyester is probably the most benign of their environmental impacts. They're made from petrochemicals in a process that uses large amounts of energy, water, and synthetic lubricants. What's more, the nitrous oxide released during the manufacture of nylon is a greenhouse gas more than 300 times more potent than carbon dioxide. When discarded (often because they smell so bad), these fabrics are stubbornly non-biodegradable.

Although manufactured from woodpulp, and so biodegradable, **rayon and viscose fabrics should also be avoided (688)**. The plantations the timber comes from often displace old-growth forests and subsistence farmers. If this weren't bad enough, the manufacturing process uses hazardous chemicals, including caustic soda and sulphuric acid. So opt for natural fabrics whenever possible.

689 **Exception to the rule** Not all artificial fibers are bad for the environment. Tencel®, the trade name for the generic fiber lyocell, is a sustainable, biodegradable textile made from the natural cellulose found in woodpulp harvested from trees grown on land unsuitable for food crops or grazing. Unlike rayon and viscose, its production process uses nontoxic, recyclable solvents. Tencel® is a versatile fiber, which can be used for clothing, upholstery, sheets, and towels.

690 **Anyone for coffee?** Next time you're after a caffeine fix, look for shade-grown coffee. The farms it's grown on support many more bird species and other types of wildlife and require much less fertilizer than full-sun plantations.

691 BOX CLEVER Buy eggs that come in cardboard boxes, not plastic ones. The cardboard boxes are usually made from recycled woodpulp and can themselves be recycled or composted—or, better still, passed to the egg stall at your local farmers' market. If you're buying lots of eggs, buy large boxes rather than lots of small ones.

692 **Convert to a cat** Catalytic converters significantly reduce the pollutants emitted in vehicle exhaust gases. They're standard equipment on new gas- and diesel-fueled cars in many countries, but if your car is more than a few years old, it may not have one. Get your local garage to retrofit this gadget.

693 **Tread carefully** Places of natural beauty inevitably attract plenty of admirers. While it can be fun to wander at will, heavy footfall can lead to soil erosion and disturb habitats, so stick to established paths to help ensure there's plenty left for the next generation to see.

694 **Be resourceful** In nature there's no such thing as waste—when it's fulfilled one function, every natural material goes on to be useful in another way. With easy access to plentiful goods, we tend to forget that fundamental principle, and we throw away an amazing 80 percent of manufactured items within six months of buying them. Think laterally—try to find as many uses as possible for everything you've bought, and throw things away as a last resort rather than an automatic response.

695 **Put another log on the fire** Burning wood isn't allowed in some areas, but elsewhere it can be an excellent low-carbon fuel if used properly. While an open fire is an attractive focal point, it's a very inefficient source of heat. So for anything more than the occasional evening blaze, use a wood-burning stove to heat your home. To keep it operating at its peak, **clean your stove thoroughly (696)** at the start of the heating season and periodically thereafter. Clear webs and other debris from the air-intake duct, inspect the chimney, and remove excess ash from the firebox on a regular basis.

Besides the condition of the stove, the type of fuel you use is important. For efficient heat production, **make sure the wood is seasoned (697)**. If necessary, store logs close to the fire for a while to dry them out thoroughly. To minimize transportation costs, **use wood from as close by as possible (698)**, and check that the forest it's cut from is managed sustainably.

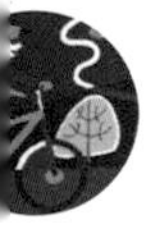

699 **Send your impedimenta in advance** Family vacations can require lots of equipment, but you don't necessarily need to travel with all of it in your car. Consider sending particularly bulky items such as bikes, surfboards, or tents ahead by train.

This will mean that your car uses less fuel, and there'll be more space for teddies, picnics, candy bars . . .

700 **Share a bicycle** If you're planning a trip to Europe, try one of the new bike-sharing programs that are springing up there, in cities such as Berlin and Rome. These cities have fleets of bikes that anyone can borrow to ride around town, picking them up and dropping them off at designated points. Some are run using special magnetic cards; others rely on simple honesty. They're a great way to enjoy quick, easy, and pollution-free sightseeing.

701 **Check the box** When you give an organization your personal details, you're often asked (usually in very small print) whether they can send you more information or pass your address on to other "selected organizations." Say no—even if part of you enjoys being deluged with torrents of junk mail.

702 **Pollution solution** When combined with heat and sunlight, car exhaust fumes form photochemical smog, which is damaging to the environment and can cause severe breathing difficulties, particularly

in asthma sufferers. Help to improve quality of life for everyone on hot, sunny days by leaving your car at home for short journeys and walking or cycling instead. A much better way to enjoy the sunshine than sitting in a traffic jam!

703 **Off-road but on-track** If you need to drive a vehicle on areas where there's no paved road, stick to established tracks to avoid excessive disturbance of plant and animal life, and soil compaction or erosion.

---

704 **A TOAST TO TOASTERS** For regular toast eaters, a toaster's a good investment, as it will use less energy than a broiler. However, if your toast habit's very occasional, it's probably not worth buying another brand-new gadget.

---

705 **Start composting at work** What happens to those few sandwiches always sitting, curling at the edges, at the end of office meetings? Whatever the nature of your place of work, it's likely that you and your colleagues amass a fair amount of compostable waste during your working day. In most cases this

goes straight into the bin for landfill, ready to produce methane, one of the most potent greenhouse gases. Talk to your office or cafeteria manager and see whether they can compost this valuable resource—either in on-site composting bins or by means of a local collection service. Each pound of rejected sandwiches, apple cores, and soggy cookies will make about 5 ounces of compost—perfect fodder for encouraging verdant plants to detox your office air (see page 20)!

706 **Cut your air con down to size** If you're buying an air conditioning unit, make sure it isn't too big for your needs. Not only do oversized units waste energy, but they're actually less effective. Air conditioners remove heat and humidity from a room by passing the air over cooling coils. If the unit is too large, it will cool the room quickly, but remove only a portion of the humidity, leaving the air feeling damp and clammy. An appropriately sized unit may take a little longer to cool a room, but it will remove humidity effectively—and use less energy.

707 **Say it with flowers** Write your next invitation, birthday wishes, or thank-you note on Grow-a-Note® paper. This beautiful handmade paper is composed of 25 percent hemp and 75 percent recycled woodpulp, infused with wildflower seeds. When your message has been enjoyed by its recipient, a few months in the soil will transform it into a patch of flowers.

708 **Beware the fatal six-pack** A few cans of beer on the beach may give you fun and pleasure, but they're not such a laugh for the birds, seals, dolphins, and other creatures who may become fatally entangled in the plastic six-pack loops often left behind after beach parties and washed out to sea. Plastic doesn't biodegrade, but after long exposure to sunlight breaks down into smaller pieces, which are fatal if eaten by wildlife. So make sure you clear up properly after your beach picnic.

709 **Be slick with your cooking oil** When you've finished frying food, don't pour the cooking oil down the drain. Besides blocking your sink, it can disrupt the water treatment process by forming a surface film, which smothers the pollution-removing bacteria. Instead, pour vegetable oil into a small container. When you've filled the container, **take it to a local restaurant (710)** that subscribes to a licensed waste-oil collection service. Animal fats can be saved to make a fat ball to feed birds (see page 205).

711 **Don't be a guttersnipe** Be careful not to drop any litter into gutters, as the next heavy rainfall will wash it into storm drains. The water that flows through these systems isn't treated, but flows directly into rivers and the sea, where your careless littering could cause all kinds of harm to the environment.

712 **LET A CORNER OF YOUR YARD RUN WILD**

Beneficial insects and small creatures such as frogs and toads love the damp, shady places created by a pile of logs in long grass, and these small garden residents will help keep pests at bay naturally.

---

713 **Yet another use for vinegar** If you've got any white vinegar left after putting it to work on your kitchen, bathroom, wooden floors, and windows, you can use it as a final rinse to remove shampoo buildup from your hair and give it body and shine. Simply rinse your hair with a mixture of one part vinegar to four parts water.

714 **City slicker** If you live in a town or city, an electric car is a great way of getting around. Batteries currently have a range of only about 30–60 miles, but that's more than enough for most urban journeys, and the technology's improving all the time. Charged from your home (ideally renewable) electricity supply, these vehicles will produce 97 percent fewer emissions than gas-powered equivalents. They'll save you a considerable amount of

money in fuel bills—and in some towns and cities, they're even exempt from parking fees.

715 **Give a gift that will grow** The ingredients can be as simple as a terracotta pot, some soil mix (ideally homemade compost), and a bulb or two. Cheaper than many bouquets, this gift will last for years, with a much lower environmental impact than hothouse flowers, which tend to be doused in chemicals and are often flown long distances only to wither within days.

716 **Gardeners' gold** Often seen as one of the nuisances of autumn, fallen leaves should be treasured by all gardeners for the rich array of minerals they hold and their superb soil-conditioning properties. Gather every last one as if they were five-dollar bills!

Left to their own devices, leaves can take up to two years to decompose, but there are two main ways to accelerate the process. First, **shred the leaves (717)** to help them break down more quickly. You don't need a special shredder to do this: just rake them into a pile on your lawn and run a rotary mower back and forth over them. When you add them to your compost pile, **mix your shredded leaves with some nitrogen-rich**

material (718), such as grass clippings, leafy weeds, uncooked kitchen waste, or manure, or a supplement, such as bonemeal. This will help activate the "cooking" process.

If you can bear the untidiness, **set aside some of your leaves over winter to shelter pest-eating insects (719)**, such as ladybugs and lacewings. Either put them in an unobtrusive pile in a corner of the patio, or spread them in a thick mulch on a portion of flower bed.

720 **On and off** Lend your support to the growing campaign to ban standby settings on electrical items such as televisions. The energy saved by this simple piece of legislation would comfortably outweigh that expended in arduous journeys from the couch to the TV set to use the on/off button.

721 **Restoration** Fight to save old buildings in your neighborhood from demolition. They represent a significant ecological investment, and even in a dilapidated state, they can still be restored and given new life using much less energy and resources than it would take to construct a building from scratch.

722 **Evergreen** For many of us, Christmas is over when there are more pine needles on the floor than left on the tree. You can alleviate this sinking feeling by buying a live Christmas tree in a pot, which you can plant in the garden afterward and maybe bring back indoors next year. **If you can't replant your tree, try to recycle it (723).** Some local governments will accept trees in January to shred for composting, and some offer a curbside collection service; just be sure to remove the tinsel first.

724 **Make your thinner go further** Whatever type of paint thinner you use, get the most out of each quart by using it several times. Simply allow the used thinner to stand in a closed, labeled container until any paint or dirt particles settle at the bottom. Carefully pour off the clear liquid into a clean container, and reuse it for your next paint job.

725 **No need for fabric softener** Beyond imparting a heady (usually synthetic) fragrance to your laundry, fabric-softening sheets do little more than reduce fabric's static cling. You can eliminate the need for this extra, potentially toxic, gunk by dampening your hands, then shaking out your clothes as you remove them from the dryer.

If the weather allows it, line-drying gets rid of static, and helps your clothes smell fresh naturally. Alternatively, **put half a cup of white vinegar in the fabric softener tray of your washer (726)** before the wash cycle. Among its many uses, vinegar is a natural fabric softener, and—despite what you might expect—won't make your clothes smell of pickles. The only thing to bear in mind is that you mustn't use bleach at the same time, as the mixture could create toxic fumes.

727 **Be a BUDDy** When you're getting materials for a do-it-yourself project, remember the BUDD rule: *buy* only what you need, *use* up everything you buy, or *donate* leftovers to a neighbor or community group, and *dispose* of waste responsibly.

728 **Wax works** Use natural waxes to bring your wooden floors and furniture to a beautiful shine. Made from wholesome ingredients such as beeswax and olive, citrus and lavender oils, they have a lovely fragrance that you may find quite addictive.

729 **CHROME FIT FOR A KING** To make your chrome fittings gleam, apply a few drops of white vinegar or organic baby oil with a cloth or sponge, or rub with the shiny side of a piece of aluminum foil.

---

730 **A marathon, not a sprint** If you're involved with a high school or college, suggest that it enters the eco-marathon—an annual competition between student teams around the world to design the most fuel-efficient vehicle possible. One school from Japan created a vehicle capable of traveling 11,195 miles per gallon! Who knows, you may help to inspire a technically minded student to design the mainstream eco-cars of the future.

731 **Food-friendly oven cleaner** You probably wouldn't consider adding commercial cleaning fluids to your cake mixture, so why spray them inside your oven? Avoid exposing your food to any toxic residues by cleaning the inside of your oven with a paste of baking soda and water. Apply an even layer and let it set for an hour, then rub it off, using light pressure with fine steel wool for tough, burnt-on stains.

732 **Café culture** Coffee grounds are full of nutrients and are particularly good for acid-loving plants, such as camellias and rhododendrons. Add them to your compost pile or just pour them directly onto the garden, where they will also act as an effective mulch. Just remember to let them cool down first, or you'll scald your plants!

For a more substantial supply, **ask your local coffee shop for their used grounds (733)**. They'll usually be happy to off-load one of their major waste products.

734 **Curb climate skepticism** If you're still skeptical about the realities of global warming, make sure you're properly informed before you make your mind up—the future of the planet could be at stake. The consensus among respected scientists worldwide is that global warming is happening, and that it's happening as a result of human activity raising levels of carbon dioxide in the atmosphere. There is evidence from around the world that climate change is happening now, and happening fast. Almost all the world's mountain glaciers are melting at unprecedented rates. The Himalayan glaciers are among the most affected—a worrying trend given that 40 percent of the world's population relies on them to provide their water.

735 **Face the truth** Watch Al Gore's documentary *An Inconvenient Truth* (2006) for more nonpartisan, hardhitting details about global warming. Take any climate-change doubters you know along with you to share your popcorn!

736 **TVs need sleep, too** If you're in the habit of falling asleep in front of the TV or while listening to music, set your appliance's sleep timer (if it has one) to switch off after a certain length of time. No performer likes to play to a snoring audience.

737 **Cleaning capsules** Try doing your laundry with enzyme "cleaning capsules." These small plastic capsules use natural enzymes to clean fabrics—a nontoxic alternative to conventional detergents. You simply toss them in with your load of laundry and refill periodically with enzyme liquid.

738 **Rejuvenate your aluminum** Kitchen utensils made from aluminum are likely to discolor, but you can brighten them by cleaning with a paste of cream of tartar and water, then buffing with a soft cloth.

739 **Truly stainless steel** Modern stainless steel fittings and appliances are the pride of many homes, but they don't look so great when they're smeared with fingermarks and spattered with grease. Resist the urge to blast your stainless steel with toxic sprays, and instead wipe it over with a cloth dampened with undiluted white vinegar—just as easy and effective, far cheaper, and (needless to say) much better for the environment.

740 **Real linoleum** The term "linoleum" has been co-opted in recent years to apply to artificial vinyl flooring that often contains harmful PVC. However, genuine linoleum is a natural, nontoxic and biodegradable product made from renewable plant-based materials—including linseed oil, which gives it its name. Always go for the real thing.

741 **Tick-tock** Choose a traditional alarm clock, which can be wound up using your own energy, rather than a digital one, which relies on electricity.

742 **Do not disturb** Wild animals are disturbed by humans across the face of the planet. We destroy their homes to grow timber to build our own houses, and poison them with our pollution. So give the poor creatures a rest when you see them in the wild. Watch and enjoy them without creating a fuss. Be particularly quiet around mothers and their young.

743 REKNIT A SWEATER Make the most of spare time while traveling, watching TV, or relaxing outdoors by knitting yourself some new clothes. This is a satisfying, low-impact pastime that's easier to pick up than to give up. Instead of buying new yarn, try unraveling an old sweater and give the yarn a new lease on life.

744 **Shiny, happy shoes** Commercial shoe polishes often contain environmentally damaging ingredients, such as trichloroethylene, methylene chloride, and nitrobenzene. Instead, rub leather shoes with olive oil and a few drops of lemon juice using a thick cotton or terry cloth rag, leave for a few minutes, and buff to a deep, natural shine with a soft, dry cloth.

745 **Share your skills** If you have a particular skill, it's likely that a charity or environmental organization in your area could benefit from it. Whether you're a tidy typist, an inspiring teacher, or a keen gardener, volunteering even a little of your time could help to amplify the efforts of local campaigners.

If you have experience or qualifications in a professional discipline, such as personnel management, law, finance, IT, marketing, or PR, you could be of great value as a board member, trustee, treasurer, or committee member. Whatever your talent, find out how you can help.

746 **Copper and brass cleaning** To remove tarnish and stains from copper or brass without harsh chemical cleaners, soak a cotton rag in a saucepan of boiling water into which you've mixed a tablespoon of salt and a cup of white vinegar. When the solution has cooled enough to handle but is still hot, rub the wet cloth onto the metal, allow it to cool, and wipe clean. For tougher jobs, sprinkle baking soda or lemon juice on the cloth before wiping.

747 **What koalas never tell you** Eucalyptus oil is a useful addition to your natural household pantry. It's an effective disinfectant and deodorizer, gets rid of stains such as ink and grease, repels certain insects, and even attacks rust.

748 **Ripple effect** A waterbed can use almost as much energy (to heat the water to a comfortable level) as a refrigerator. As there are 17 million of them in the United States alone, this is bad news. If you're one of those who likes literally to float into unconsciousness, you can reduce the amount of energy your waterbed uses by insulating it on all sides. If you cover the bed with a quilt as soon as you get up, this will also help keep heat in.

749 **Natural glide** Try using castor or mineral oils to lubricate switches and hinges around the house instead of lubricants containing toxic solvents.

750 **Reload your printer** Reconditioned toner cartridges are made to international standards and are available from major computer and stationery outlets as well as supermarkets and chains. Buying reconditioned cartridges helps save valuable resources (each laser cartridge that's recycled conserves the equivalent of around a quart of oil), and will cost you less than cartridges made from virgin plastic.

751 **Good enough to eat** If you need to use disposable plates and dishes for a big event, serve food on biodegradable, compostable dishes and flatware made from cornstarch, sugar cane, bamboo, or tropical leaves. That way, you'll end up with a big pile of worm fodder that will soon be valuable compost, rather than a stack of landfill.

752 **Lower-energy printing** If you need to buy a printer for your home or office, try to make it an inkjet model, as these use about a sixth of the energy that laser printers get through. **If you need to buy a laser printer, look for one with an energy-saver feature (753)**. This reduces energy use when idle by more than 65 percent.

754 **Go blank** Computer monitors use approximately 90 watts of power when they're on (even when screensavers are operating), but only a few watts when they're in power save, sleep, or hibernate modes. So make sure your workstation isn't gobbling energy unnecessarily when your back's turned by switching your screensaver setting to "none" or "blank screen."

755 **Laundry revolution** You can eliminate chemicals from your laundry routine by using "eco-balls," or "laundry balls," instead of detergent. These Saturn-shaped spheres contain magnetic pellets, which produce ionized oxygen, enabling the water in your machine to penetrate deep into your washing and draw out dirt, while softening fabrics at the same time. Fans claim that the only things eco-balls won't do that detergent and fabric conditioner can are provide an artificial fragrance for your clothes, irritate your skin, fill up your cabinets, and empty your wallet.

756 **Clean and fresh** To get pungent smells such as onion, garlic, or fish off utensils and chopping boards, wipe them with vinegar and wash in soapy water.

757 **Stuck for gift ideas?** You're not the only one. Literally billions of dollars are spent each year on unwanted gifts. So instead of another set of scented soaps or pair of novelty socks, give something that will really last. Some charities offer a range of gifts you can give to developing countries on behalf of your loved one—from a goat, pig, or chicken to a water purification system. **Sponsorship or adoption of an endangered species (758)** is a great gift for children. Alternatively, **dedicate a tree (759)** or area of forest to someone you love—a gift that will probably outlive them.

760 **ESCAPE FROM THE DAILY GRIND** Kitchen sink garbage disposal units need lots of water to operate properly, and add considerably to the volume of solids in septic tanks, which can lead to maintenance problems. Instead of putting your garbage down these revolting contraptions, put it to good use in a compost pile or wormery (see page 215) instead.

---

761 **Police your polystyrene use** Polystyrene is a ubiquitous part of convenience culture, cropping up in everything from disposable coffee cups to fruit wrappers, egg boxes, and packing cases. This synthetic material is made from valuable petrochemicals and doesn't biodegrade, so try to use it as little as possible. If, despite your best efforts, you do build up a stockpile, **find out whether any recycling centers in your area accept polystyrene (762)** for recycling. Some do, but most don't—because it's so bulky, transportation and processing are prohibitively expensive.

763 **Herbal hair happiness** The secret of healthy hair may lie a few feet away in your garden. You can make your own completely natural hair treatments for free from common herbs and plants. For example, **use lavender or thyme to tackle dandruff or an itchy scalp (764)**: boil four tablespoons of the dried herb in a pint of water for ten minutes, let the decoction cool, then work it into your scalp (having dampened your hair), and leave for an hour before rinsing. **Use rosemary in the same way to stimulate hair growth or condition dark hair (765)**.

766 **Nothing's perfect** Energy-saving compact fluorescent lightbulbs (CFLs) do have one drawback, which is that they contain mercury, a toxic metal that evaporates easily and can travel long distances in the atmosphere, contributing to local, regional, and global pollution. This means that it's particularly important not to put CFLs into your general trash, because the bulbs would almost certainly break, releasing the mercury. Fortunately, they can be recycled in a controlled process that stops the mercury from escaping. If your local government doesn't accept expired CFLs for curbside collection, ask it to do so in the future. Meanwhile, take them to your nearest recycling center. Bearing in mind how much longer CFLs last than traditional incandescent lightbulbs, this isn't a trip you'll need to make very often.

767 **Give natural bouquets** Flower growing has become one of the planet's most pesticide- and poison-intensive agricultural activities. Many cut flowers are doused with insecticides, fungicides, and growth regulators, and fumigated with methyl bromide, which is toxic to humans and depletes the ozone layer.

So protect growers, the environment, and your lover's nostrils by giving sweetly scented organic Fairtrade flowers. Better still, grow your own, or give a potted plant for longer-lasting pleasure.

768 **Outdoor learning** Modern (particularly urban) environments are often devoid of dedicated places for children and young people to explore and enjoy nature. Help to redress the balance by encouraging your local school or community group to develop outdoor learning centers in your neighborhood or on school grounds. To begin with, try creating a discovery trail, butterfly garden, sundial, weather station, acid-rain monitor, bird hide, pond, or interpretation materials. Make sure you get the children who'll be using the facilities involved in making them so they end up with something they really like and cherish.

769 **Ethical insurance** Next time you need to take out car or travel insurance, get a quote from one of the increasing number of providers that pay carbon offsets (see page 373) on your behalf according to the distance you travel.

770 **Careful with your antifreeze** Most antifreeze contains ethylene glycol. This is toxic to start with and becomes even more so as it picks up toxic substances such as benzene and lead from your car's engine. Keep this lethal mixture tightly sealed in a safe place, as it's deadly to animals and children, who might be attracted by its sweet taste. Never pour used antifreeze into your trash can, down drains or sewers, or onto the ground. Instead, take it to a recycling center or hazardous waste depot, or ask your local service station or car dealer if they can deal with it. **Look for propylene glycol-based antifreeze (771)**, which is less toxic than the commonly used ethylene glycol versions.

772 **A word or two about motor oil** Check that you're using the right type of oil for your car's engine: if the oil's too viscous, the engine's moving parts will be meeting more resistance, and therefore using more fuel, than necessary. **Change the oil every 3,000–5,000 miles (773)** for optimum efficiency, making sure that the old oil is recycled.

When motor oil needs changing, it's not because the oil itself has worn out, but because it has become contaminated with particles that reduce its effectiveness. Used oil can be re-refined, which removes all these contaminants and leaves it as good as new. So, next time your car needs an oil change, **ask for re-refined oil (774)**. Stringent tests have proved that it performs just as well as virgin oil.

775 **Get in gear** If you drive a car with a manual gearshift, the way you handle the gears can have a significant effect on fuel consumption. On the open road it's best to get up to top gear as soon as possible, but without accelerating harder than necessary. However, once you're in top gear, don't stay in it at all costs—letting your engine labor can be just as uneconomical as heavy acceleration, so change down when going uphill or around corners. If you're driving an automatic, ease back slightly on the accelerator once the car gathers momentum to allow the transmission to shift up smoothly.

776 **Check your air filters** Clogged air filters can reduce your car's efficiency, making it use up to 10 percent more fuel than necessary. So keep the filters clean, and replace them regularly.

777 **On the boil** Rethinking the way you use the cooktop can save time and energy. Simple measures include: **putting lids on saucepans (778)** to stop heat from escaping; **selecting a pan no bigger than required (779)** for the amount of food you're cooking and a burner no bigger than the pan, and **chopping up food into smaller pieces (780)** so that it cooks more quickly. And get the most out of each burner's energy by doubling or tripling up: **cook several items on top of each other in a stacked steamer (781).**

782 **Become a Freecycler** The idea behind the international Freecycle movement (see page 372) is simple: members receive for free things they need but don't have that other members have but don't need. This internet-based "free cycle" of goods is facilitated by local volunteers, who help turn users' trash into treasure, keeping thousands of useful items out of landfill sites.

783 **Take part in an aquatic cleanup** Find out what local conservation groups are doing to clean up water habitats in your neighborhood, and lend a hand cutting back excess vegetation and removing trash from the water and the banks of streams, rivers, ponds, and lakes. When the hard work's over, take your friends back for a visit to enjoy your handiwork and watch the area flourish.

784 **Look after your car and it'll look after you** Make sure that you service your car regularly. A poorly tuned engine can use up to 50 percent more fuel and produce up to 50 percent more emissions than one in peak condition. Most vehicles manufactured since 1996 are equipped with an "on-board diagnostic system" (OBD), which measures engine function. **Don't ignore your car's "check engine" light (785)**: this is the OBD's way of telling you there's a problem that's causing increased air pollution and reduced fuel economy, so take it to a qualified technician as soon as possible. The sooner you act, the easier (and cheaper) it'll be to repair the fault.

---

786 **CELEBRATE EARTH DAY** Since 1970 each year people around the world have celebrated the planet on 22nd April—Earth Day—through a variety of individual and community activities. Take part in some of the events organized in your area (see page 370), and renew your commitment to help protect our living planet.

---

787 **Be label-conscious** When you're shopping, take time to read the small print. An increasing number of product labels not only list ingredients but also provide indicators about environmental performance. Look for products that are approved by independent certification boards, such as the Energy Star, FSC, or the European Eco-label (a small green flower with blue stars as petals), which guarantee that a product has a lower environmental impact than other comparable ones.

788 **Dress to impress** Try making your own mayonnaise. Once you've sampled its fresh, vibrant flavor, you'll be very reluctant to return to preservative-laden commercial varieties. Beat two egg yolks and mix them with three-quarters of a teaspoon of salt, half a teaspoon of mustard powder, and four or five teaspoons of lemon juice or white wine vinegar. Then, beat in 1 to 1½ cups of olive oil, a drop at a time, making sure that each drop has been absorbed into the mixture before adding any more. To reduce the slim risk of salmonella associated with eating raw eggs, make sure that you use very fresh ones, keep your mayonnaise refrigerated, and use it within three days—if you've got any left, you can always put it on your hair (see page 295)!

789 **Change of axis** If you need to replace your top-loading washing machine, make your next one a front-loader. Front-loading machines use less water and, therefore, energy (because most of the energy is used to heat the water) than top-loading models. They also require less detergent and wash more thoroughly.

790 **Pick your moment** Whenever possible, plan your car journeys for times of the day when there's likely to be little traffic. Not only will you get to your destination more quickly and in a better mood, but you'll save fuel: stop-start driving is less economical than serene progress at a steady speed.

791 **Saving money all the time** By leaving your car at home, you'll of course shell out less on fuel. But now infrequent drivers can also save money on their car insurance: look for a company that offers a "pay as you drive" policy. The lower your mileage, the lower your premium. Studies suggest that the more people who pay their car insurance this way, the better it will be for the environment. When this pricing method was piloted by an insurance company in the United States, participating drivers reduced their mileage by an average of 20 percent.

792 NO FLY ZONE Give bottles, cans, and other containers a quick rinse before putting them in the recycling bin. This will help stop them from attracting flies both at home and at the recycling center.

793 Don't let your pool be a water hog Private swimming pools use a huge—and some would say unjustifiable—amount of water. But if you look after your pool actively and responsibly, you can minimize its environmental impact. **If you've got an outdoor pool, keep it covered (794)** when not in use. This will reduce water loss due to normal evaporation, insulate the water against overnight heat loss, and keep the water cleaner, reducing the need for chemicals and filtration. **Check for leaks by monitoring the water level each week (795)**. If it drops by more than normal, you may well have a leak: find it and deal with it as soon as possible. Left unrepaired, a leak causing the water level to drop by just an inch a day in a 10ft.-by-30ft. pool would waste more than 60,000 gallons per year. To confirm or allay your suspicions, **conduct a bucket test (796)**. Fill a bucket with water, and leave it next to the pool (with the cover off) for 24 hours. Mark the water level in both pool and bucket. If, after 24 hours, the water has gone down more in the pool than in the bucket, you have a leak. (If the level in the bucket has gone down more, you have a hole in your bucket!)

Another worthwhile water-saving measure is to **fill your pool with rainwater (797)** rather than drinking-quality tap water.

This can be achieved using a simple collection tank and filtration device connected to your roof.

798 Make sure your bird food doesn't create cat food To make sure any birds using your garden aren't easy prey for feline stalkers, keep bird feeders at least 6 feet away from dense vegetation, where hunting cats might lurk, and nesting boxes well out of cats' reach.

799 Flat battery? The average lead acid car battery contains nearly 18 pounds of lead and more than 2 quarts of sulfuric acid, which are both dangerous to human health and the environment. So it goes without saying that car batteries should always be reclaimed or recycled. Trade in your old battery when you buy a replacement, or take it to a local salvage yard or recycling center.

800 Choose a sparky gas range When you're choosing a new gas stove, look for one with electronic (piezo) ignition, which should use about 40 percent less gas than a model with a pilot light.

801 GO FOR A RAMBLE There are few more pleasant ways of spending a bright, crisp winter's day than rambling through some beautiful countryside. Make sure you're having minimal impact on the environment you're enjoying by leaving your car at home. This way you don't have to walk back to where you parked, but can walk to a more distant destination and get the train or bus home.

---

802 Organize your generosity Instead of giving randomly to environmental charities, set up regular automatic transfers to your favorite causes. This will help you and the charity to plan ahead financially—and, of course, you may be able to claim a tax deduction on these gifts.

803 Tip-top laptop If you need to buy a new computer, consider a laptop instead of a desktop, as it will consume up to 90 percent less energy. Make sure you choose one that can be upgraded and has a long life expectancy, and invest in a robust bag to protect it when you're working on the go.

804 **Freshen up your home** Banish mildew from shower curtains and other damp spots around the house with undiluted white vinegar, applied using a sponge or a spray bottle. Leave as long as possible before rinsing. If you don't like the vinegary smell, open the window or burn some essential oil nearby until the smell's worn off.

805 **Put your hand up** Look for volunteer programs that enable you to help improve social or environmental conditions overseas. Some require a considerable commitment. The Peace Corps, for example, places people with professional skills in teaching, management, social work, health care, and IT in posts for two years. If you haven't got that much time to spare, or are unsure whether you have relevant professional expertise, other organizations offer shorter placements, from as little as a week. You should gain fantastic insights into life in different cultures, and skills that will be useful in future life, and possibly have the chance to make a real difference.

If you'd like to help, but have responsibilities at home that prevent you from relocating, **consider joining the UN online volunteering program (806)**. This network links computer-savvy volunteers with agencies and projects that need help with work that can be undertaken over the internet, such as translation, programming, and writing business or marketing proposals.

807 **A room with a view** For sparkling windows without side effects, clean panes inside and out with a mixture of ½ cup of white vinegar to 3 cups of warm water applied with a spray bottle. Use a squeegee to remove excess liquid, and buff the window dry with a soft cloth or newspaper. It often takes a couple of applications for a completely streak-free finish, as the waxes in any commercial products you may have used previously take some time to remove.

808 **Expensive luxury** Using a vehicle's air conditioner can increase fuel consumption by more than 20 percent in city driving. Unless the weather's unbearably hot, use the flow-through ventilation on your car instead. Opening the windows is another option, but only at speeds below 45mph. Above this speed, open windows not only inconvenience toupee wearers but also cause aerodynamic drag, reducing fuel efficiency.

809 Strength in numbers Join forces with those who feel the same way as you about an environmental or social issue by signing—or starting up—a petition, and delivering it to the decision-makers you'd like to influence.

810 Mole control Moles can damage a garden by producing unsightly molehills in the middle of the lawn and by literally undermining plants with their shallow tunnels, which cause roots to dry out. On the plus side, they feed on slugs, and their burrowing produces crumbly soil that's great for potted plants.

Conventional methods of control, such as trapping, fumigation, and poisoning, are inhumane, environmentally harmful, and usually ineffective. Instead, **try a solar-powered sonic mole deterrent (811)**, which emits vibrations through the ground to keep our velvety friends at bay.

812 Rescue mission Feel like you're stuck in a concrete desert? Think again. Even the busiest city can be home to a multitude

of wildlife. Connect with the nature in your neighborhood, and help it to thrive by giving your time to an urban wildlife rescue organization. You'll be amazed how many unseen habitats there are on your block.

813 **DON'T FEED WILD ANIMALS** It can be very tempting to try to make contact with wild animals by giving them food, but doing so can make them less wary of humans than they perhaps should be, and dependent on them for food—and can adversely affect their health. So, apart from garden birds, which can be safely fed with nuts and seeds (see page 370), don't feed wild animals, and make sure any stored food and garbage are kept out of reach of potential scavengers.

---

814 **Going postal** The average household accumulates far more rubber bands than it can possibly use. However, your local postal sorting office may use them for batching mail. Next time you're clearing out your kitchen drawers, treat your postman to an elastic bonanza.

815 **Low-water shaving** Instead of rinsing your razor under running water, use a few inches of warm water in the basin. This will rinse your razor just as effectively, using far less water.

816 **Expand your Fairtrade repertoire** The range of Fairtrade goods is growing fast. This socially equitable method of trading enables producers to meet their basic food, health, housing, social security, and education needs. The environment also benefits, as the Fairtrade Foundation uses its influence to promote eco-friendly methods of production. In order to continue growing, the market needs active support from consumers. So try to add at least one new Fairtrade item to your shopping cart each month.

817 **Flag drag** If you feel strongly enough about a particular cause to fly a flag, don't attach it to your car. It has been calculated that a car parading two small flags would create enough drag to burn up to an extra quart of fuel for each hour that it traveled at an average of 65mph. Make your feelings known with a bumper sticker, or fly a flag from your house instead.

818 **Tackle your damp problem** If you've got a problem with damp or humidity in your home or office, try installing a solar-powered dehumidifier. This ingenious device ventilates, warms, and dehumidifies buildings using only the power of the sun, and so it has no running costs.

819 Natural sunscreen The chemicals in standard sunblock can be absorbed through the skin and expose the body to free radicals, which can increase the risk of cancer, and excess estrogen, which can disrupt sexual development. Instead, choose sunscreens based on plant-derived ingredients, such as aloe vera, jojoba oil and green tea. They work just as well as mainstream products, but without such potential side effects. Alternatively, to enjoy completely unprocessed sun protection from a plant, **relax under the dappled shade of a tree (820)**. You'll reduce the need for lotions and allow your skin slowly to build up some natural resistance to the sun. **Cover up with a wide-brimmed hat and light shirt (821)** when you need to make forays into bright sunlight, and stay indoors during the hottest part of the day.

822 Help Nelly the Elephant say goodbye to the circus
If you want to visit a circus, make sure that the only performers playing the clown are human ones. Humane conditions for circus animals are rare, and in some countries the beasts are taken straight from the wild.

823 Organic growth Drawing heavily on nutrients to fuel their rapid development, babies and children are particularly affected by the content of their food. So to give them the best possible start and protect them from the health risks associated with exposure to pesticide residues, try to feed your children organic food whenever you can—even if the rest of the family is still on the conventional stuff.

824 **Nest in peace** Birds are threatened by habitat destruction worldwide, and populations of more than a third of the world's 1,200 species are decreasing. If you're lucky enough to have birds nesting in your garden, take care not to disturb them, and never remove eggs from nests—the mother may well be nearby, but is likely to abandon her eggs if they've been touched.

---

825 **KEEP YOUR PAWS OFF** However cute the wild animal you're admiring, you should never try to touch it. You could be carrying diseases to which it isn't immune, and it could return the favor—along with a scratch, bite, or sting.

---

826 **Trojan horse** Don't bring plants or animals home from your holidays. Releasing nonnative species into the environment can be disastrous, as they may carry disease or dominate local species.

827 **Keep your copper** Copper is 100 percent recyclable in an efficient process that requires only 15 percent of the total energy consumed in mining, milling, smelting, and refining the virgin metal. So it's worth taking any old copper items, such as wires or piping, to a recycling center. (Copper alloys, such as bronze and brass, can also be recycled efficiently.) You may even be paid for your contribution.

828 **Avoid canine chaos** If you're visiting wildlife habitats with your dog, keep it close to you—on a leash, if necessary—to ensure that it doesn't disturb birds and other creatures. Even if your dog doesn't kill them, it might disturb their feeding or nesting sites.

829 **Run!** Running is a free, carbon-neutral way of getting fit. All you need is a pair of running shoes, so get out there and enjoy the great outdoors. If you need some extra motivation, **enter an organized race and collect sponsorship for a planet-saving cause (830)**. Start off with a local fun run, and if you enjoy it you may just find yourself in a marathon in years to come. Just remember to recycle your running shoes when they wear out.

831 **Keep your recycling dry** To avoid moisture contamination and mold buildup, try to keep your recycling dry until it's collected or you take it to the local recycling depot. If you don't have space indoors, try to cover containers kept outside.

832 **Om comforts** Practice yoga on a mat made from a natural, organic, and recyclable material such as rubber, cotton, or hemp. They absorb your sweat, don't slip, and can be cleaned and washed easily. They're a much better option than the vast majority of today's yoga mats, which contain PVC. This is considered to be the most toxic of all plastics—just what you want to avoid when you're realigning yourself physically, spiritually, and mentally to look after yourself and the planet.

833 **Daily discoveries** Help your children's connection with nature to flourish rather than wither by introducing them to a different nature-based activity every day. If you're running out of ideas, try looking at a book of nature games and activities tailored to the seasons for inspiration (see page 368).

834 **Take your children camping** Eating, sleeping, and generally having fun in close contact with the natural world can help to build a lifelong love of, and respect for, nature. Take advantage of good weather to empower your child with a sense of self-sufficiency and a love of the earth. Replace the usual distractions, such as toys, cellphones, CD players, and magazines, with binoculars, identification books, wood-carving knives, compasses, and magnifying glasses, so that your children are well armed to interact with whatever they discover. If you're feeling extra adventurous (and the weather's nice), **make your own shelter out of whatever natural materials you can find (835)**, and spend a night sleeping in its protection. You may want to take a waterproof tarp with you, just in case . . .

836 **Divide and conquer** Make your good recycling intentions easy to stick to by devising a simple system for sorting and storing your waste. Find out what materials your local recycling center or collection service accepts, and set up an appropriate storage bin system in your home. Have a labeled container for each type of waste in your kitchen so that putting things into them is as quick and easy as putting them into a mixed trash can. Bins with built-in dividers are now available in lots of shapes and sizes—either free-standing or incorporated into a kitchen cabinet—so your kitchen needn't be crammed with a whole line of new containers.

837 **Time is money** Whether your roof needs tiling, your lawn mowing, or your furniture restoring, find out whether there's an HOURS branch in your community. The HOURS program, launched in Ithaca, New York, in 1991, now operates in many American communities. It uses locally produced paper currency to pay for locally produced goods and services. Besides giving members access to services that might otherwise be beyond their financial means and supporting local businesses, the HOURS concept helps communities to protect themselves against environmentally destructive overdevelopment by big business.

838 **Stick to your list** Before you leave home, make a shopping list of all the things you need to buy. Ideally, keep one on the kitchen wall so you can add things as you run out. This will help you to buy only what you need and avoid all the impulse purchases we're encouraged to make in large stores and supermarkets.

839 **Feed your follicles** If you're rustling up a batch of homemade mayonnaise (see page 275), make a bit more than you need and use what's left to nourish your hair—it's particularly good for brittle hair. Work in about ½ cup of mayonnaise while your hair's dry, leave it to set for 15 minutes, then rinse thoroughly and wash as usual. If you're between mayo-making sessions, **try a mixture of mashed avocado and coconut milk (840)** instead, using the same method.

841 **Take your hot water on a short cut** If you're planning a new home or renovation, make sure that your water heater is installed close to where hot water is going to be needed most often. However well insulated your pipes, heat will inevitably be lost as water moves along them, so don't make it travel via too many detours!

842 **DANGLE YOUR DOG A CARROT** Reduce your dog's ecological pawprint by feeding it less meat. Producing meat puts a heavy strain on the environment (see page 30). Unlike cats, which need a certain amount of meat, dogs can thrive on a vegetarian diet. Vegetarian dog food contains all the nutrients needed for canine health and can be supplemented by scraps (including the occasional piece of meat or bone) from your family meals.

---

843 **Become a TV multitasker** Only got one eye on the TV? Use your couch potato interludes as a chance to mend clothes, sharpen knives, or even fix your bike. Properly maintained, your possessions will last longer (and with a "productive viewing" policy you may find you limit your junk-viewing hours).

844 **Take a tint hint** Many hair dyes contain harsh chemicals such as peroxide, ammonia, diaminobenzene, and p-Phenylenediamine (PPD). Studies indicate that these substances are harmful both to the environment and to humans. The chemicals can enter the

skin of the scalp, and regular usage has been linked to cancers of the bladder, blood, and lymph. To avoid these nasties, try coloring your hair with natural tints made from henna and other eco-friendly substances. If you feel you really can't live without harsher chemical dyes, at least try to reduce the frequency of applications.

845 A rose by any other name
Avoid perfumes and cosmetics scented with rosewood or pau rosa, which are extracted from the Brazilian rosewood tree. Overharvesting of rosewood (a key ingredient in some famous perfumes) has almost completely eliminated this plant from the Amazon. Instead, look for products scented with sustainably harvested botanicals or essential oils.

846 Exert your influence In the highly competitive world of retail, companies depend on the value of their brand and a favorable public profile. Although it can take time, manufacturers and retailers do respond to negative publicity over their environmental and social performance. So if you're unhappy about how a particular organization goes about its business, make an effort to join (or start) a campaign for change. The results could be dramatic . . .

847 **Cast-iron guarantee** When you're investing in a new saucepan, choose one that will last. Cast iron becomes naturally nonstick with use and is the most durable cookware around, so you'll keep it forever.

848 **Techno-nap** Next time you go for a break at work, give your computer one as well. Set it to enter power-saving mode after five minutes of inactivity. It'll revive almost instantly with the touch of a key when you're back at your desk.

849 **Free-wheeling vacation** Once you've reached your vacation destination, try renting bicycles instead of the usual rental car. The rest of your explorations will be carbon-neutral, you'll save some cash for sampling local delights, and you'll have a chance to burn off any you might enjoy to excess!

850 **USE THE SUN'S POWER** Every two minutes the sun gives the Earth more energy than we use in a year. Photovoltaic (PV) technology, which turns solar energy into electricity, is developing at a dazzling rate—global PV energy production has increased by an average of 28 percent per year since 1993. Make sure your electricity provider is exploiting this infinite resource, and consider supplementing your power supply by installing PV panels on your roof.

---

851 **Switch it off** Do you need your microwave oven to tell you the time? If not, turn it off completely when you're not cooking with it. The average microwave, in active employment for only a tiny fraction of the day, uses more energy to power its digital clock than to heat food.

852 Living bouquets Use potted plants in place cut flowers as centerpieces on the tables at any events you stage. You can give them to your guests at the end of the party, or take them home to enjoy for months or even years.

853 Watch your screenwash Take care not to spill windshield-wiper fluid onto the ground or pour it down the drain, as the antifreeze it usually contains is poisonous (see page 270). Except when you need your wipers to cut through ice, homemade fluid, made from three parts white vinegar mixed with one part water, is an effective nontoxic alternative.

854 Don't drown your food Unless you're going to use the cooking water to make soup, save energy by using only enough water to cover the food that you're boiling.

855 Dispose of smoke detectors smartly While invaluable in helping to safeguard your home, smoke detectors that work by ionization contain a small amount of radioactive material. They are completely safe unless the chamber in which the

material is held is broken. This obviously means that ionization smoke detectors should be disposed of very carefully. When your detector no longer works, return it to the manufacturer, or take it to your local waste recycling center. Alternatively, **install photoelectric smoke detectors (856)**, which don't contain any radioactive material.

857 **Mix and mismatch** The manmade substances contained in cosmetics and toiletries are often tested only individually, and we don't know what effect exposure to a "cocktail" of different products will have on us or the environment. If you use a variety of synthetic cosmetics and toiletries, try to minimize the number you use and avoid mixing them if at all possible.

858 **Use a trailer** If you need to move outsize loads around by car, it's usually better to put them on a trailer rather than a roofrack (this may not be practicable for unwieldy items, such as ladders). Trailers—particularly lightweight aluminum ones—are more aerodynamic: you'll get through up to 15 percent less fuel than if you used a roofrack.

859 **Read between the lines** More and more skin and hair products are being marketed as "organic." But read the label carefully: unlike organic food, organic cosmetics and toiletries aren't rigorously policed. Some manufacturers may be guilty of overstating the eco-friendly credentials of their products, describing them as "organic" even if only a tiny proportion of the ingredients have been produced organically. To avoid being hoodwinked by such "greenwashing" practices, **look for certification by a reputable organization (860)**, such as the National Organic Program in the United States or, in Britain, the Soil Association. These two bodies allow only products with at least 95 percent organic ingredients to be certified as "organic."

861 **Don't be a dipstick** If your car drips oil onto the street, the oil washes into storm drains and then into local waterways. A gallon of motor oil can contaminate a million gallons of water, so make sure you don't contribute to this problem: regularly check your levels and look for leaks under your car. If you do find a leak, get it fixed promptly—and in the meantime **catch the oil with a drip pan (862)** when your vehicle's parked, and dispose of it at a recycling center.

863 **CHILD'S PLAY** Why not start a toy library? Get together with other like-minded parents and contribute slightly used toys and games to start the collection. The system works along the lines of a book library and will give your child and others access to more toys than you can afford to buy. Or, if you just want to recycle those that have lost their appeal, **donate toys to a local doctor's office, hospital ward, or thrift shop (864)**.

865 **Petal power** Replace harsh and astringent skin toners with rose water, which is 100 percent natural, and has great skin-softening properties. To make your own, steep some rose petals in hot water until their fragrance has infused the liquid. Remove the petals, and store the rose water in the fridge, where it will keep for up to a week, or pour it into an ice-cube tray and use straight from the freezer. If that sounds too much like hard work, you can buy rose extract from gourmet stores.

866 **A low-carbon future** Radical measures to curb greenhouse gas emissions by rationing individuals' carbon use are being developed by some governments. One plan under consideration involves awarding each of us an identical annual carbon allowance, which could be stored as points, similar to frequent flier miles or supermarket loyalty points, on an electronic swipe card. Points would be deducted at point of sale for every purchase closely related to non-renewable energy, such as gas or air tickets. People who didn't use their full allocation, such as members of families who don't own a car, would be able to sell their surplus points to a central bank. People who exceeded their allocation could then draw the relevant number of carbon points from the bank, with the cost added to their utility bills. The overall number of points available nationally would steadily decrease each year.

Prepare for the introduction of any such plan by setting yourself a carbon target that's lower than your current carbon footprint (see page 17), and reduce it further next year.

867 Make your own face mask Instead of buying fancily packaged facial masks, try making your own from organic, preservative-free ingredients. Mix a teaspoon of clear honey (which is full of vitamins and has antiseptic qualities) with two teaspoons of plain yogurt and a teaspoon of oats. Gently rub the mixture into your face, leave to dry for 15 minutes, then remove with a hot, damp cloth. The yogurt will cleanse your skin, and the oats provide gentle exfoliation.

868 **HARVEST THE RAIN** To cut the amount of tap water your family uses by up to half, consider investing in a rainwater harvesting system. This collects the rain that lands on your roof and filters it for use in your toilet, washing machine, garden, or swimming pool. While still relatively expensive to retrofit, these systems add little to the cost of a new home, and you'll quickly recoup any additional outlay by saving on water bills.

869 **Give your dishwasher a boost** Next time you need to buy a new dishwasher, look for one with a booster heater, which (if necessary) raises the temperature of the water used to wash dishes within the machine itself, whenever you run a wash. This means you can turn down the thermostat on your home's water heater, saving energy and money. Any extra cost of the dishwasher should be recouped by energy savings within a year.

870 **Brown and green** Sunbeds can endanger both your health and that of the planet. Each sunbed contains around 45 energy-hungry tanning lamps, which each hold four times the amount of toxic mercury found in a normal fluorescent tube, causing major disposal problems. Save energy, avoid mercury waste and protect your skin from premature ageing and an increased risk of melanoma by boycotting sunbeds in favor of a natural self-tanning lotion containing plant-derived DHA (the active ingredient in self-tanning products that causes your skin to go brown). Or take the edge off your pallor by applying a natural sunblock and going out in the sun for short periods (see pages 288–289). It's much more pleasant, and you'll top up your body's vitamin D reserves (available from natural light) at the same time.

871 **Coming to a screen near you**

Liquid crystal display (LCD) screens are currently the most energy-efficient on the market. But a new contender could soon join the low-energy viewing arena: organic light-emitting diodes (OLEDs) can be used to illuminate screens using much less energy than other technologies. Still in their infancy, OLEDs are currently used only in cellphones, but should soon be developed for use in televisions and computers.

872 **Tidy fridge** Clear out your fridge regularly to minimize the amount of food and drink it has to keep cool. By keeping the fridge tidy, you can find what you're looking for quickly. Up to 30 percent of the cool air escapes every time you open the fridge, so the quicker you can grab stuff and close the door the better.

873 Make them work for your vote
If you're fed up with seeing streetlights left on in daylight or empty public buildings lit up at night, ask your local politicians to make sure that they're leading by example and show that public facilities are making real efforts to cut their energy use, generate their own renewable energy, and generally green up their act.

874 Simmer down Unless there are lots of people using your coffee maker on a regular basis throughout the day, there's no point in leaving its "keep warm" function on for long periods. Turn it off at the plug when you've made your morning brew, or it will use enough energy to make 12 more cups before you decide to have another in the late afternoon.

875 **MAKE A POSITIVE DIFFERENCE** "If many little people in many little places do many little deeds, they can change the face of the Earth" (African proverb). Never underestimate the impact of your actions.

---

876 **Need a reminder?** For up-to-date facts and figures on the state of the planet, consult the Worldwatch Institute's *Vital Signs* and *State of the World* reports. They should galvanize you into action!

877 **Healing action** In the 1980s scientists discovered that manmade chemicals were destroying the ozone layer that protects us from the sun's most damaging rays. Governments around the world quickly adopted the Montreal Protocol (1987), which banned ozone-destroying gases such as chlorofluorocarbons (CFCs)—found in aerosol cans, fridges, and air conditioners.

Since then, levels of the most critical CFCs have stabilized or declined. There's still a significant ozone hole over Antarctica, but elsewhere the ozone layer seems to be on the mend. This healing may not be attributable solely to the Montreal Protocol, as sunspots, volcanoes, and weather also play a role in regulating ozone levels. But it suggests that concerted action to repair our mistakes is possible. If the trend continues, the ozone layer should be restored to 1980 levels by 2070. By then, even the Antarctic ozone hole might have closed—for good.

878 **Visit an eco-village** Communities of people striving to live sustainably are springing up across the world. With any luck, one day they'll be as common as today's suburbs—but in the meantime, if you don't know of one near you, contact the growing global eco-village network (see page 373) for information, news, resources, courses, and educational programs.

879 **Age of excess** "Earlier periods in human history were marked by the material that distinguished the era—the Stone Age and the Bronze Age, for example. Our age is simply the Material Age, an age of excess, whose distinguishing feature is not the use of any material but the sheer volume of materials consumed." (Lester R. Brown, the Worldwatch Institute, in *Eco-Economy*).

880 **Write away** "The Earth is not dying—it is being killed. And the people who are killing it have names and addresses." (U. Utah Phillips). If you're worried about environmental issues, let your concerns be known in a letter to the people responsible. Besides writing individually, **join a letter-writing campaign (881)**, such as one organized by Global Response (www.globalresponse.org) to help communities stop environmental destruction.

882 **Any color—so long as it's green** If you need to buy a new car, try to make sure that it's better for the environment than the last one. **Go for a manual gear transmission (883)**, if possible, as these are 10–15 percent more fuel-efficient than automatic models. If you don't feel confident driving manually, take a refresher lesson or two to learn the basics. **Choose the smallest car that will fulfill your regular needs (884)**. For example, do you really need an SUV if you're the only person in it for most of the year? Might it be more sensible to buy a small car for your daily needs and rent a bigger one for your annual vacation? **Study comparative fuel-consumption data (885)** in order to identify the most efficient model in the size class you want to buy.

If you normally drive a gas-powered car, **consider switching to diesel (886)**. Diesel engines are 20–40 percent more economical than gas engines, and recent models are quieter and emit much lower levels of pollutants than older versions, which makes this fuel a relatively clean choice. If you have an older diesel-burning car, switch to bio-diesel, made from used cooking oil. Bio-diesel and other new fuel technologies (see pages 141 and 336) offer the ultimate in efficiency—if all goes well, it won't be long before they become the standard in mainstream vehicles.

887 Relocate a frog family If you've got a well-appointed garden pond (with plenty of vegetation and sloping sides for easy amphibian access), carefully collect a small amount of frog spawn from a local pond, along with a bucket of pond water, and transfer it to your pond to provide a new home for the emerging tadpoles. Make sure that you leave plenty of frog spawn in the place you found it. Cats like hunting frogs, so fit your pet felines with an easy-release bell collar (see page 80).

888 **Stock option** If you have ethical concerns about the way a particular company operates, consider becoming a shareholder. Even if you own just one share, you can attend the company's annual meeting, where you can raise questions about issues that trouble you. You also have a right to vote on the company's major decisions (although if your stake is tiny, this would have an impact only as part of a wider campaign). Major corporations are increasingly being held to account in this way on issues ranging from environmental destruction to waste disposal, child labor, and dubious sales techniques.

889 **Recycled steel's a steal** Look for products made from recycled steel—from paperclips to garden tools and building materials.

890 **Beer can save the planet** Most manufacturing byproducts do nothing but harm to the environment. However, in brewing the opposite is the case. Beer bran, a byproduct of brewing with barley, can be used to remove pollutants such as benzene from industrial waste, keeping them out of rivers and lakes. So, to support your local ecosystem, support your local brewer.

891 **Catch some rays** As well as appearing on roofs worldwide (see page 300), solar panels are being incorporated into a variety of portable products, thanks to the invention of a discreet, lightweight photovoltaic unit known as the "power pocket." **Equip yourself with a solar backpack (892)** with built-in power pockets, and you'll be able to charge your cellphone, MP3 player, and other micro-devices while you're on the move.

893 Don't lapse into long-distance

The lure of the exotic can be hard to resist, but an intercontinental long-distance flight can produce more CO_2 emissions per passenger than the average motorist does in a year—an easy way of undoing all your good deeds at home. So before you book a far-flung trip, investigate vacation options closer to home. You may find far more variety than on a package trip farther afield.

894 Cut CO_2 on your doorstep The average American home is responsible for emitting 23,000 pounds of CO_2 a year. Try to introduce at least one domestic energy-saving measure each month over the next year to reduce your home's contribution.

895 **Try mentoring** If you're looking for inspiration about how to live or work differently, try to find a mentor to help you fulfill your potential. If you'd like to give something back, you can make a real difference to someone else's life by becoming a mentor yourself. You'll never stop learning . . .

896 **Build with bamboo** Bamboo is often overlooked by builders and designers, but this versatile material is stronger than steel in tension and concrete in compression, and has many uses around the home, from flooring to framing. It's pretty useful while it's growing, too, acting as a bio-absorber to clean pollutants out of the soil, preventing erosion, and returning more oxygen to the air through photosynthesis than almost any other deciduous plant.

897 LEARN SECRETS FROM THE OLDER GENERATION

Take time to talk to your grandparents or great-grandparents about how they used to live. Experts on doing more with less, they lived without many of the features of modern life that are causing environmental problems today, and may have excellent suggestions for how you could reduce your environmental impact while maintaining a good quality of life.

---

898 Hot drinks using natural fuel

Rather than using a polluting camping gas stove, equip yourself with a storm kettle to provide naturally heated hot drinks when you're out in the wild. Fill the kettle with water, put small dry twigs, wood, or pieces of scrunched-up scrap paper in the base, light them, and in five minutes you'll have 2½ pints of boiling water.

899 **Task lighting** Does the whole room need to be ablaze with light to illuminate you reading a book in one corner? If not, switch off the overhead lighting and snuggle up next to a lamp. If a million homes all reduced their average electricity load by just 60 watts (one incandescent lightbulb), they'd cut carbon emissions by around five million tons a year.

900 **Energy-free refrigeration** If you don't need to keep many items cool—for example, milk for a small office—try making your own fridge. Take two unglazed terracotta flower pots of different sizes, and stack them together with a layer of wet sand between. If you keep the sand wet and cover the top with an old towel or blanket, the interior of the smaller pot should stay cool, as the evaporating water transfers heat energy into the air. You may find you no longer need a conventional electric fridge at all, in which case make sure your old one is recycled properly. If that's too radical a move, keep your energy guzzler unplugged except during the hottest months.

901 **A new way to clean** Microfiber cleaning cloths are designed to attract dirt without the need for any cleaning product—chemical or otherwise. They can be used dry, or dampened with a little water. When used damp, the cloths clean all surfaces, including glass, stainless steel, plastics, chrome, brass, wood, and ceramics. When used dry, they have a natural positive charge which attracts dust. Simply wash them with the rest of your laundry when they get dirty, and use again—hundreds of times.

902 **Turn your boss into a green guru** Faced with the daily stresses of running a business, your chief executive may consider the "greenness" of your workplace a peripheral matter. If so, it's your job to persuade him or her otherwise—not least, by showing them how much they can cut overheads by implementing simple energy-saving measures, such as a computer-shutdown policy.

Instead of putting the onus on your boss to take action, volunteer your own time: **circulate energy-saving tips (903)**, either by "all-staff" e-mail or company message board, and **invite suggestions from your co-workers (904)**. When it becomes clear how much money you've saved your company, it may be not just the environment that benefits, but also your career.

905 **Make your own paper** Put yourself at the business end of recycling: set aside some old newspapers and magazines to make your own paper (see page 372). You can even use leaves from the garden. This is a simple though somewhat messy process that's great fun to do with children and produces uniquely patterned and textured art paper. You'll probably be able to find all the equipment you need in your kitchen, so get pulping!

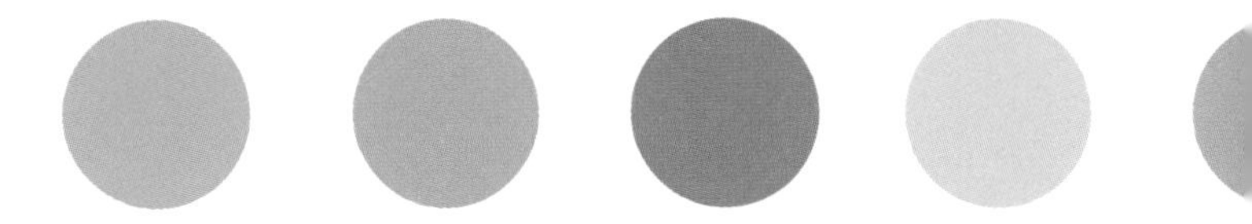

906 **ANY EXCUSE FOR A PARTY** Why not host a clothes-swapping bash? Ask guests each to bring along a bag of decent-quality clothes they no longer want, keep donations anonymous (as far as possible), agree to ban the taste police, and provide plenty of refreshments to keep people's changing-room stamina fueled.

---

907 **Get some advice about eco-friendly investments**

If you're not money-minded, thinking through investments can be daunting at the best of times. If finding out about ethical and environmentally positive financial products seems too much like hard work, enlist the help of a specialist financial adviser to help you navigate interest rates and returns that respect your ethical priorities. Alternatively, try an ethical research service website for suggestions (see page 371).

908 Fund your home with green Your home may be the single biggest investment you make in your life. So make sure your financial commitment is achieving the best possible result for the planet by using a green mortgage. These range from light to dark green options. Some of the darker green ones won't lend you money unless your property will give an ecological payback. Other green mortgages provide incentives such as discounts on your mortgage rate when you carry out eco-improvements, planting trees every year to offset the emissions created by your home, or donating money to environmental charities.

909 Cotton on to organic Only 2.5 percent of the world's farmed land is used to produce cotton, but more than a quarter of the world's pesticides are poured onto these crops, making them the most polluting—and polluted—on the planet. So buy organic cotton whenever you can—it's appearing in more and more clothing collections.

910 **Soup up your veggies** Mixed-vegetable soups, such as minestrone, are a great way to get the most out of leftovers or any vegetables that just need using up. Tops of scallions, celery and cabbage hearts, and tomatoes too ripe for salads can be thrown in. Leftover pasta, potatoes (even mashed), rice, and legumes can go in, too. If you **freeze leftovers as you go (911)**, there's always something in the house to make a nutritious meal from.

912 **Bean bags** Save aluminum and other resources by buying dried lentils and other legumes rather than canned ones. They're much lighter and less bulky to transport, as well as being much cheaper to buy. **Soak dried legumes for as long as possible (913)**—ideally between 12 and 24 hours—to reduce the time, and therefore energy, needed to cook them. A teaspoon of baking soda in the soaking water can help soften tough skins.

914 **Taming the vending machine** Left to its own devices, the office hot-drinks machine could hardly be described as the greenest of inventions. However, it can be brought into line. For example, **encourage co-workers to fill up with a mug (915)**, rather than a disposable plastic cup, and provide spare mugs for visitors to use. You could also **ask your office manager to stock the machine with organic tea, coffee, and hot chocolate (916)**. These can now be bought for vending machines and are available at competitive prices.

917 **Drip, drip, drip** Just one leaking faucet can waste up to 8 gallons of water a week—enough for a shower. So replace the washer as soon as you hear that tell-tale drip.

918 **Give it a rest** Unless you happen to be a doctor on call or the president of a nation in crisis, remember to switch off your cellphone before you go to bed. This will save battery power and stop you from being woken up at four in the morning by a text message offering you free ring tones.

919 **Give swordfish the chop** Swordfish has been overfished for the past century or more, and stocks are now at the lowest level on record. Most of those for sale are caught before they've had a chance to breed, so depleting stocks further. Forgo this fishy treat in favor of other less threatened species (see page 223).

920 **FROM FIELD TO FORK**

To ensure that your food is as fresh as possible, buy direct from the person who produced it. Shopping in farm shops or at farmers' markets also guarantees the best possible return for the farmers, rather than most of their profits going to supermarkets.

---

921 **Blankets on the menu** If you're eating alfresco at a restaurant or café in the company of a propane-gas patio heater, ask the staff to switch it off (check this is OK with other diners). Suggest that the restaurant get rid of these energy-hungry contraptions and instead provide blankets for diners to drape over themselves.

922 Identify your real needs In an age of abundance, we're inundated with ever-more crazy opportunities to spend money and consume more. Sophisticated marketing is designed to persuade us we need to have more and more stuff in order to be happy. Some luxuries undoubtedly make life pleasant, but many are little more than gimmicks. So when you're tempted to jump on the next gizmo bandwagon, ask yourself whether you really need this latest ecosystem-plundering indulgence. Seventeen million heated toilet seats have already been sold worldwide, and the Japanese manufacturer is hoping to sell 400,000 a year to North America alone. Maybe it's time for a reality check.

923 Join the real-world gym A fit body is the ideal vehicle for a healthy, fulfilled life. But staying in shape can seem like one chore too many when your life's already full. Save yourself time and money by turning your back on the gym and its energy-hungry exercise machines, and try some of the following real-world workouts instead.

Take the stairs (924): you'll get shapely buttocks, while saving the energy required to power the elevator. **Walk, run, or cycle to work, shops, and to see friends (925)**. Tone your arms, shoulders, and back: **collect your shower- or bathwater in a bucket (926)** and carry it out to water the garden. Or **chop wood for your fireplace (927)**. For a productive weight-training session, **walk your recycling to the nearest collection center (928)**—and if you still yearn for the burn, you could offer to take your neighbors' waste on a separate trip.

929 **Don't get heated up for hot plates** If you're using the oven to cook a meal, you can heat up the plates you're going to eat it from by putting them on the bottom rack for the last few minutes of cooking—just turn the oven off and use the heat that's collected. But if you're not using the oven to cook, don't waste energy by turning it on just to warm the plates. Instead, place them over the saucepan you're cooking in, and cover with a cloth.

930 **Good tide-ings** The energy held in the oceans' tides, waves, currents, and temperature differentials can be tapped for human use. Most such technologies are still at the experimental stage, but several sizable and successful tidal-power installations are already in place, and Scotland and Australia are among a growing list of countries investing in ocean-energy technologies.

931 **TAKE TO THE HIGH SEAS** If your appetite for long-distance travel won't subside, instead of going on several short trips by plane, try saving up your leave and going on a longer, potentially more rewarding trip by boat. You can even **travel by freighter (932)**, which will be cheaper than a cruise, take you to places the average tourist never sees, and dramatically slash your journey's carbon emissions.

933 Home brew If you're partial to a brew or two, spare the environment the cost of manufacturing, transporting, and disposing of hundreds of beer cans and bottles by treating yourself to your own homemade organic beer at a fraction of the cost of commercial brands. You can buy a full brewing kit for less than $150—the only thing you need to provide after that is water. Once you get the hang of it, you'll soon be experimenting with different techniques and ingredients—and it's a perfect excuse for a tasting party . . .

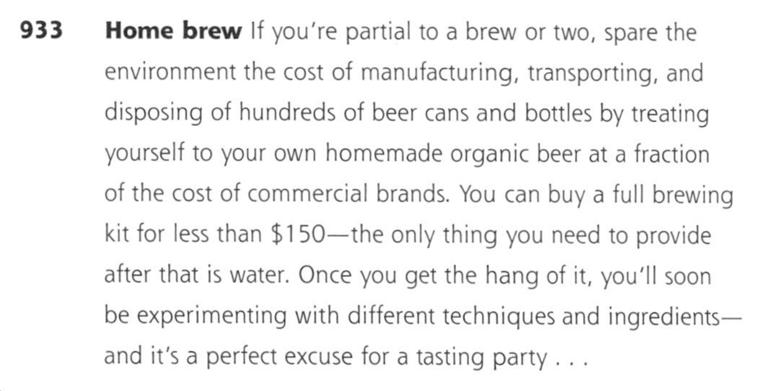

934 **The wheel of the year** Phenology is the recording and study of annually recurring natural events, such as the first sightings of species of migratory birds or the first ripening of wild fruit. Climatologists and ecologists find such data invaluable in monitoring climate change year on year and region by region. Every one of us can help in the gathering of this information by taking time to notice and report seasonal phenomena near our homes to a national phenological survey (see page 370).

935 **Clean set of wheels** If you're buying a new car, there has never been a better choice of mainstream alternatives to conventional gas- or diesel-fueled models. Consider, for example, gas-electric hybrids, which can travel 55 miles or more on a gallon of gas. You can probably even **convert your existing car to run on cleaner fuel (936)**, such as LPG (liquefied petroleum gas) or bio-diesel, often made from vegetable oil. Bio-diesel is carbon-neutral, as the carbon dioxide emitted in its combustion is offset by the growth of new crops planted for its production.

937 **Say no to GMOs** Genetically modified organisms (GMOs) have had their genetic makeup altered in a way that doesn't occur through normal breeding, in order to give them certain features, such as disease immunity or resistance to pests or drought. Not all the risks associated with these methods have yet become clear, but it seems that the impacts on human and environmental health could be very high. Many GM crops currently grown are bred to resist a broad-spectrum herbicide that would kill their non-GM counterparts. This leads to a huge increase in agrochemical use, which has a devastating effect on the local ecosystem. To avoid these products, look for food labeled GM-free (see pages 360–361), buy certified organic produce (which can't contain GMOs), and **let suppliers know that you're not happy about their stocking genetically modified food (938)**.

939 **Walnut wonders** Conceal scratches in wooden furniture naturally with the oil from crushed walnuts. The result won't look as pristine as a brand-new finish, but will add to the character of pieces that bear the brunt of a busy life.

940 **Self-preservation** To avoid the potentially detrimental impact of synthetic preservatives such as parabens (see page 56) in your toiletries and cosmetics, choose self-preserving organic products such as moisturizing body oils made from cocoa butter or sunflower, peppermint, coconut, or spearmint oils. They last naturally for up to 18 months.

---

941 **SPA TREATMENT** Besides feeding the birds in your yard (see page 205), remember that they also need water—both for drinking and for bathing. Get a birdbath and keep it filled with clean water—preferably rainwater from a rain barrel. It's best to change the water daily and give the bottom of the bath a quick rinse to prevent the spread of disease.

---

942 **Say goodbye to prewashing** Modern washing machines are so efficient that the prewash cycle is generally unnecessary. If your clothes are really dirty, leave them to soak for a while before putting them in the machine. Avoiding the prewash setting will cut each load's energy use by 15 percent.

943 **Have a smaller family** This is a difficult subject to broach, but population growth is one of the biggest challenges to achieving sustainability. Over the last century the human population has grown from one to six billion (while life expectancy has doubled), and it isn't expected to stabilize until about 2100, when there'll be about 11 billion people on the planet. Meanwhile, every year each of us consumes more of the world's resources and produces more waste. Since 1972 we've been using the planet's resources at a rate faster than it can replenish them, and most (86 percent) of that bounty supports the lifestyle of the richest 20 percent of the population. If the developing world follows our example of how to live, the planet will face even bigger challenges. So while we each work on reducing our environmental impact, it would help if we had fewer children, perhaps adopting more often. If, over the next 50 years, each family had only one child, the population would return to six billion by 2050.

944 **Get your kids gardening** However many children you have, the garden is a great place for them to interact with nature in a meaningful and rewarding way from an early age. They'll

quickly learn what plants and creatures need to thrive (and that they don't need so-called "miracle" pesticides and fertilizers), and they'll gain a great sense of achievement from watching the things they tend grow and flourish—and maybe even provide them with some meals and snacks. If possible, **give your children their own patch of garden to tend (945)**—a raised bed, some containers, a ground plot, or even a disused sandbox. Set them up for success by making sure that their area's right in the middle of the action, with the best soil and light, and giving them proper gardening tools—scaled down, if necessary. Let them choose what they want to do with their plot, but gently **steer them toward crops that are relatively easy to grow (946)**, have short growing seasons, and are fun to harvest, such as radishes, cherry tomatoes, sunflowers, sugarsnap peas, carrots, and pumpkins.

947 **Wave goodbye to dirty beaches** When you're planning a daytrip or vacation to the coast, look for beaches awarded a Blue Wave (Blue Flag in Europe) for good water quality management. Support from tourists will encourage accredited beaches to maintain their standards, and may persuade managers of unaffiliated ones to clean up their act.

948 **Shade your home with some leafy vines** If you live in a hot climate, shading is the simplest, most effective way to cool your home and reduce energy consumption. Train quick-growing vines up trellises on the hottest side of the house to provide an attractive source of shading and cooling. Make sure the trellis is kept at least 6 inches from the building to protect the wall and provide a buffer of cool air. If there's no open soil around your home, climbing plants such as deciduous clematis and wisteria grow well in containers. Ask your local nursery which plants are best suited to your climate and needs.

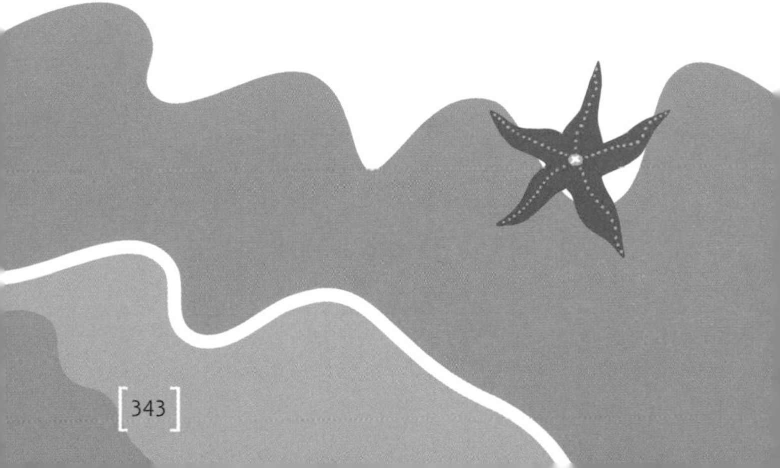

949 **Summer sleeping** Hot air rises, so if your bedroom's stuffy in hot weather, try sleeping downstairs (if your home has more than one story), rather than using air conditioning or a fan. Failing that, **create a cooling evening breeze (950)** by opening a window in your bedroom and another in an adjoining room.

---

951 **FORGO A FANCY FRIDGE** When choosing a new fridge, remember that the simpler the model, the better for the environment. Avoiding snazzy extras like auto defrost, ice makers, and heaters to control condensation can cut the fridge's energy use and running costs by up to 60 percent, and should also make it cheaper.

---

952 **Cook a solar meal** For zero-impact cooking, try making a meal in a solar oven (if the sun's out). These portable devices are probably the most energy-efficient cooking appliances available, as they require no fuel of any kind to cook, yet allow you to bake, boil, or steam food in about the same time it would take on a normal stove. They're ideal for picnics or camping trips—particularly in areas where fires are prohibited. In fact, there's no reason why you shouldn't turn your yard into a carbon-neutral outdoor kitchen throughout the summer! For rainy days or cooking at night, hybrid versions with an energy-efficient electric back-up are also available.

953 **Little wonders** LEDs (light-emitting diodes) are small, solid, extremely energy-efficient lightbulbs. Until recently, they were available only in single-bulb applications, often on electronic gadgets, but they're now available in a variety of guises. They last ten times as long as compact fluorescents, and a massive 130 times longer than typical incandescent bulbs, and use a fraction of the wattage. Look for LED products such as flashlights, Christmas lights (see page 148), headlights, and small task lights.

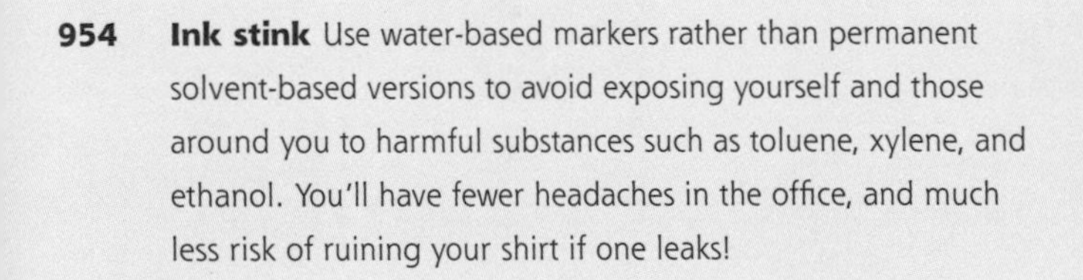

954 **Ink stink** Use water-based markers rather than permanent solvent-based versions to avoid exposing yourself and those around you to harmful substances such as toluene, xylene, and ethanol. You'll have fewer headaches in the office, and much less risk of ruining your shirt if one leaks!

955 **Look for EcoSpun clothes** Next time you need a durable item of clothing, look for EcoSpun, a high-quality polyester fiber made from recycled plastic drink bottles. It's used to make fabrics such as fleece, and can be blended with other fibers, such as wool, cotton, and Tencel®, for clothing as well as carpets and home furnishings.

956 **Fair reward** If you've got a sweet tooth, reward yourself for your efforts to live a sustainable lifestyle by enjoying a bar of organic Fairtrade chocolate. Besides offering a better deal to its producers, Fairtrade cocoa is one of the most environmentally friendly tropical crops, as it is generally grown with minimal use of pesticides and fungicides.

957 **Overload** The more work you ask your car to do, the more fuel it'll use. So make sure it's not lugging unnecessary weight around by clearing out the trunk regularly.

958 **Accidents will happen** Banish stains from rugs and upholstery using a splash of soda water or a mixture of equal parts water and white vinegar. Sponge the offending mark off as soon as possible after it has formed.

959 **THE MORNING AFTER** If you suffer from hangovers after drinking wine but not other forms of alcohol, you may be sensitive to sulfur dioxide, a preservative added to wine that is believed to contribute to allergic reactions such as rashes and headaches. Try switching to organic wines, which typically contain, at most, half the sulfur dioxide of nonorganic ones.

---

960 **Go topless** Plastics are notoriously difficult to recycle because there are so many different types, which can't be mixed. When putting PET plastic bottles to one side to be recycled, remember to take the caps off, as these are made from a different polymer and need to be recycled separately.

961 **Don't be a two-fridge household** A surprising number of homes have a second "backup" fridge or freezer. If you're a chiller-heavy household, think about how much food you really need to keep cool at one time. If you really do need a lot of chilling space, **get one large refrigerator (962)**: this will be cheaper and more efficient to run than two smaller ones. But it's likely that you're actually storing much more food (and cold air) than you really need. Try running down your supplies and making do with just one refrigerator, buying fresh food more regularly if necessary. You can always **keep the second fridge in reserve (963)** and just plug it in when the extended family comes for a long stay.

964 **Support your local stores** Many small-scale food retailers go out of business every year in the face of relentless, loss-leading competition from supermarkets. This can create "food deserts" in our town centers. Rather than driving miles to a supermarket, try shopping more regularly at local independent shops—while you still can. You'll help reduce the pollution generated by trips to strip-mall supermarkets, and give a much-needed boost to your local town center.

965 **The nuclear debate** Nuclear energy generates almost as much heat among those who argue about it as it does in our homes. Its supporters see it as the only way at present to produce low-carbon energy on a large scale. They fear that if we carry on using coal, oil, and natural gas at current rates until renewable sources are capable of meeting our needs, global warming will have become irreversible in the meantime.

Opponents of nuclear power argue that if we invested as much in research into new forms of energy as it costs to run nuclear facilities, renewable energy would soon be widely available. They believe that we can't justify running the risk of an accident at—or terrorist attack on—a nuclear power station, because such an event would be so devastating. Even when a nuclear plant operates normally, it emits radioactive pollution, which can travel long distances. Nuclear reactors also produce waste that remains harmful for thousands of years, causing chronic storage problems.

As a consumer, you can take a stand: **investigate the sources of your supplier's energy (966)** and change provider if you don't like what you discover.

967 Get paid to save the planet

A growing number of organizations in almost every sector now employ people specifically to help improve their environmental performance. If you'd like to reduce environmental impact from within, consider applying for one of these jobs and use your position to influence real change. If the organization you currently work for doesn't have an environmental officer, suggest that it creates such a post (you may need to suggest that the organization first creates an environmental policy, if it's really behind the times), then submit your application.

968 Make powerful pen pals To have the mandate to make change happen, decision makers in government often need to be able to demonstrate that the electorate wants them to do something. Provide politicians with the support they need to make difficult decisions by sending regular postcards advocating the causes you believe in—whether reducing carbon emissions or ensuring cleaner oceans. There may be organized card- or letter-writing campaigns that you can join to amplify your efforts.

969 Joint venture Offices waste millions of tons of paper each year, yet this material is easily recyclable. There's probably a local or national collection company that will deal with your office waste paper, but if you have difficulties finding one, try setting up a recycling cooperative with other businesses in your area. By talking to your commercial neighbors about recycling, you may even find you can do business with them in other ways. Communication is always a good thing.

970 Eco-exchange Bring the waste-reducing ethos of the Freecycle movement (see page 273) to your workplace, school, or place of worship by setting up a local eco-exchange bulletin board—online, if possible (more impact, less paper). Users would be able to advertise leftover products, such as paint, oven cleaner, or building materials, in the hope of finding a good home for them.

971 The trouble with farmed fish You might think that buying farmed fish is a sensible response to the problem of overfishing wild fish (see page 223). However, most fish farms only make things worse. Large-scale, intensive farms plunder huge amounts of wild fish for meal feed (about 30 pounds to produce a 6-pound farmed salmon), which also denies seals and sea birds their natural food source. Fish kept in high-density pens are vulnerable to disease, so they have to be dosed with bucketloads of antibiotics, which can leach into surrounding water and enter the food chain. And when farmed fish escape, as they often do, and breed with their wild counterparts, the natural immunity of the wild population is compromised.

Fortunately, a new breed of fish farmers who recognize the impact that aquaculture can have on the environment is emerging. If you buy farmed fish, **look for fish from low-density, organic farms (972)** that respect the local ecosystem.

973 **Don't get in a lather** Try to avoid using more detergent than you actually need to get your clothes clean. Not only does overdosing waste the resources and energy used to make the detergent, it also makes your washing machine work harder, and requires extra processing to clean up the washing water once it leaves your machine. Follow the dosage instructions on the soap's packaging, and experiment to see whether you can get good results using less (the manufacturer may want you to err on the generous side). You could also **contact your water company to find out how hard or soft your home's water supply is (974)**. Many people overestimate the hardness of their water and end up using far too much detergent.

975 **OUT OF SIGHT** A tried-and-tested way to satisfy the demands of young children for new toys is to put some of their existing ones away in the attic every so often when they've grown bored with them, and then bring them back out in a few months' time. Your children will greet their new-old playthings like long-lost friends.

976 **Shades of meaning** Many items are now labeled as "recyclable" with a "mobius loop" triangle of arrows on a light background: ♲. Most things could theoretically be recycled, but buying these products still puts the onus on you to make them available for recycling. Instead, try to choose items made from materials that have already been recycled. These are marked with a mobius loop on a dark background: ♻. A subtle difference on the label with a big impact on the environment.

977 **Blue bottles are no longer a nuisance** Blue bottles (of the glass rather than insect variety) can, in most places, be recycled in the same system as green ones, so put them in the green container at your local glass-recycling center.

978 **Red, yellow, and, above all, green** Many cities, particularly in the United States, are replacing incandescent bulbs in traffic signals with LEDs (see page 345), because they use 80 percent less electricity. Find out whether your local government is considering making this switch, and, if not, lobby them to do so. They'll not only save on running costs but will need to change the bulbs much less often.

979 Don't shell out for turtle meat Humans are marine turtles' biggest enemies. Threatened by hunters of their meat, eggs, and shells, and by pollution caused by human activity, six out of the world's seven species of marine turtle are at risk of extinction, despite having been protected internationally since 1990. Help these beautiful animals to survive by refusing turtle meat and turtle products if they're ever offered to you as a local delicacy, and support organizations that protect turtle breeding grounds.

---

980 RECYCLE YOUR CAR If your old jalopy is unsalable, take it to a registered scrapyard for environmentally sound dismantling. Even the most beaten-up wreck probably still contains valuable working parts, and about three-quarters of the material of the car will be recyclable. The majority of this is steel, which can be efficiently and cost-effectively melted down and reused many times over.

---

981 Curb your can consumption Seventy-five percent of the millions of canned drinks sold each day come in aluminum cans. Mining aluminum causes severe environmental damage, then smelting it uses huge amounts of energy: worldwide, the aluminum industry uses as much electric power as the entire African continent. So try to choose drinks in refillable glass bottles. Or, even better, mix your own soft drink in a reusable bottle. If you need to grab a can, make sure you recycle it, as recycling aluminum saves 95 percent of the energy needed to make a new can.

982 **Kick-start your compost** If you haven't got a garden or your garden's too small for a full-size compost heap, try *bokashi*—a traditional Japanese system for fermenting organic matter to create fertilizer. Its modern incarnation enlists the help of "effective microorganisms" (EM) to ferment food waste and other organic matter in a speedy "pickling" process. Equip your kitchen with an air-tight *bokashi* bucket. Every time you throw in waste food scraps (including cooked food—even meat and fish), sprinkle in a handful of the EM-infused bran supplied with the bucket, and in a few weeks you'll have nutrient-rich soil improver to dig into your garden (or window-box), and fertilizer juice from the bucket's tap—great for your houseplants.

983 **Rewire without PVC** If your home's due to have its electrical wiring replaced, take advantage of the opportunity to get rid of all the PVC that's likely to be covering it. Polyvinyl chloride (PVC) is the world's second most commonly used and most environmentally harmful plastic. Luckily, it's easy to replace with benign insulating material, so ask your electrician to help detoxify your whole electrical system.

984 **An ocean apart** North America and Europe are divided by more than just the Atlantic—the two continents also have markedly different approaches to the labeling of genetically modified (GM) foods (see page 337). In the European Union, foods produced with GM ingredients have to be labeled as such, so that consumers can make an informed choice. No such requirement exists in the United States and Canada, the world's biggest producers of GM foods. However, there's a groundswell of opposition to genetic engineering in these countries: a 2003 survey showed that 55 percent of Americans and 63 percent of Canadians objected to GM foods. To register your opposition to genetically modified foods, **write to your congressman and your representative in your state legislature and press**

for labeling regulations (985). Better yet, organize a petition and get as many signatures as you can.

986 **The Great Warming** For a fast-track look at climate change and possible solutions, watch *The Great Warming* (2003). Filmed in eight countries on four continents, endorsed by dozens of the world's leading scientists, this three-hour Canadian television series is one of the most factually accurate, visually stunning, and wide-ranging productions ever mounted on this complex, fascinating subject.

987 Chop on a bamboo board

As an alternative to buying a chopping board made from tropical hardwood, look for one made from bamboo. This fast-growing, sustainable, and versatile material is extremely durable and naturally antibacterial, withstands regular washing, and is a beautiful detail for your kitchen.

988 Mail-order happiness If you can't get the products you need locally, buying goods online can be an eco-friendly and time-saving way to shop. When buying from the cyber-aisles, try to **plan ahead so that you don't need to demand super-fast delivery times (989)**. More flexible postal arrangements allow distributors to run delivery trucks at full capacity and to use more fuel-efficient forms of transportation, such as train and boat. To save on postage and unnecessary journeys, and to take advantage of bulk-buy deals, **combine orders with friends, relatives, or colleagues (990)**. If your home is unoccupied for most of the day, **have orders delivered to your workplace (991)**, where they can always be accepted—this avoids having to re-send items, or your having to make awkward and fuel-consuming trips to the delivery depot, if you're not home when they arrive.

---

992 **COOK SOME MULTI-MEALS** If you're going to the effort of cooking from scratch, try preparing enough for two or three meals, and freezing or refrigerating what you don't want that day (remembering to let the food go cold before you chill it). You may need to chop up a few extra vegetables, but you'll dramatically reduce the amount of energy you and your oven have to put into the second and third meals—and many foods taste better reheated.

---

993 **Take the venom out of your rum punch** Rum is made from sugar cane, which is often heavily sprayed with pesticides. So next time you're rustling up a Caribbean cocktail, use organic rum.

994 **Crunch time** Lower your breakfast cereal's carbon footprint by dousing it in organic milk, which uses only a third of the energy needed to produce its nonorganic counterpart.

995 **Everything under one lid** Save time and energy in the kitchen by preparing whole meals in one pot. For example, try boiling rice in a large covered pan, then adding a layer of vegetables, plus strips of meat or tofu, and steaming them. Dishes based on potatoes or pasta can be prepared in a similar way, as can traditional stews and pot roasts. Whatever the recipe, a one-pot meal will generally use about a third of the energy of a meal cooked in separate pans.

996 **Medicinal effect** If you've bought or been prescribed medicine that you no longer need, instead of leaving it to fester in your bathroom cabinet until it's expired, pass it on to a humanitarian organization (see page 372) that can redistribute it to some of the thousands of people who die every day because they don't have access to proper medical care.

997 Face-to-face shopping Before supermarkets, shopping used to be a far more sociable experience. Rediscover the friendlier way to shop by buying your groceries over the counter from specialist food stores—or, failing that, from the deli counter at your supermarket. That way, you can ask for exactly the amount that you need, making it less likely that food will go to waste, and bypass the hermetically sealed plastic packaging to be found in the aisles.

998 Back-door GMOs If you want to avoid eating genetically modified organisms (GMOs), you can look for food that is labeled GMO-free (see page 360) or certified organic. But if you eat meat or animal products, you may be eating GMOs unknowingly, as there's currently no requirement anywhere in the world to label products from animals that have been fed on GM feed. If you don't want to be exposed to GM crops by this indirect route, write to farmers and food distributors, asking them to keep GM crops out of animal feed.

999 Celebrate a cigarette-free life If you manage to give up smoking, celebrate by planting a tree every year on the anniversary of your last puff—or have one planted on your behalf (see page 65). Each year, nearly 500,000 acres of woodland are destroyed to make way for tobacco plantations. Now that your lungs are getting cleaner, it's time to return the favor by helping to replenish the planet's lungs.

1000 Quick thinkers avoid fast-food When you're on the go in an unfamiliar area, it can be hard to find somewhere healthy to eat, particularly if you've got hungry children in tow, with their finely tuned pester powers. Try to avoid succumbing to the ubiquitous junk-fuel stations by keeping a supply of healthful snacks in your bag, such as mixed nuts, seeds, and dried fruit, to stave off hunger pangs for long enough to find a place that'll serve you a decent meal. You'll avoid the intensively and pollutingly mass-produced food served by fast-food chains and the mountains of nonrecyclable packaging they produce. And you and the environment will be healthier for it.

1001 Sail into the sunset Capturing the wind's energy in a sail is a wonderfully low-impact way of getting around. If you don't happen to own your own yacht, you can still explore the oceans on a zero-carbon vessel by helping to crew a sailing boat. Scour ads in sailing magazines for opportunities, and get ready to head for the Bahamas. (It might be a good idea to have a few sailing lessons first!)

FURTHER READING

Christensen, K. *The Armchair Environmentalist*. MQ Publications, 2004.

Clark, D. *The Rough Guide to Ethical Shopping*. Rough Guides, 2004.

Drake, J. and Love, A. *The Kids' Summer Games Book*. Kids Can Press, 2002.

Duncanson, A. *Ecology Begins at Home*. Green Books, 2004.

Hacker, R. *How to Live Green, Cheap and Happy*. Stackpole Books, 1994.

Hickman, L. *A Good Life*. Transworld Publishers, 2005.

Khaneka, P. *Do the Right Things*. New Internationalist Publications, 2004.

Lawrence, F. *Not on the Label*. Penguin Books, 2004.

Milord, S. *The Kids' Nature Book*. Williamson, 1996.

Petrini, C. *Slow Food*. Columbia University Press, 2001.

Reay, D. *Climate Change Begins at Home*. Macmillan, 2005.

Scott, N. *Composting*. Green Books, 2006.

Sullivan, K. *Organic Living in 10 Simple Lessons*. Barron's Educational Series, 2001.

Various authors. *Recycle*. Black Dog Publishing, 2006.

Worldwatch Institute. *Vital Signs*. Norton, published annually.

Young, W. *Sold Out – The True Cost of Supermarket Shopping*. Vision Paperbacks, 2004.

USEFUL WEBSITES

General information

The Ecologist online magazine (www.theecologist.org)
Friends of the Earth (www.foe.org)
Global Green USA (www.globalgreen.org)
Greenmatters (www.greenmatters.com)
Greenpeace USA (www.greenpeace.org/usa/)
Worldwatch Institute (www.worldwatch.org)

Babies and children

Green Schools Program (Alliance to Save Energy)
(www.ase.org/section/program/greenschl)
Institute for Earth Education (www.eartheducation.org). *Learning resources.*
La Leche League in the U.S.A. (www.lllusa.org). *Breastfeeding.*
National Association of Diaper Services (www.diapernet.org). *Reusable diapers.*
U.S.A. Toy Library Association (www.usatla.home.comcast.net)
Wastefreelunches.org (www.wastefreelunches.org)

Biodiversity and ecology

American Evergreen Foundation (www.usagreen.org). *Volunteer to take part in environmental projects.*
Earthwatch Institute (www.earthwatch.org)

Environmental Protection Agency (www.epa.gov)

Forest Stewardship Council (www.fsc.org)

National Audubon Society (www.audubon.org). *Advice on feeding birds.*

Rainforest Foundation (www.rainforestfoundation.org)

Wildlife Trust (www.wildlifetrust.org)

World Land Trust (www.worldlandtrust.org). *Buy a section of rainforest.*

World Society for the Protection of Animals (www.wspa-usa.org)

Climate change

Earth Day Network (www.earthday.net). *Includes Ecological Footprint Quiz.*

National Phenology Network (www.uwm.edu/Dept/Geography/npn/). *Report natural seasonal changes to help monitor climate change.*

Safe Climate (www.safeclimate.net). *Calculate your carbon footprint.*

Consumer and shopping

Eco Business Links (www.ecobusinesslinks.com)

Eco Mall (www.ecomall.com)

Environmental Working Group (www.ewg.org). *Includes guide to ingredients of cosmetics and toiletries.*

Ethical Junction (www.ethical-junction.org)

Fair Trade Certified (www.transfairusa.org)

Local Exchange Trading Systems (www.lets-linkup.com). *Find a LETS group near you.*

Energy

Alliance to Save Energy (www.ase.org)

Department of Energy (www.doe.gov)

Eartheasy (www.eartheasy.com)

Energy Star (www.energystar.gov)

The Green Power Network (www.eere.energy.gov/greenpower/). *Change to a green electricity supplier.*

Rocky Mountain Institute (www.rmi.org)

Windustry (www.windustry.com). *Learn how to harvest the wind.*

Ethical living

Ethical Investment Research Services (www.eiris.org)

Ethical Wills (www.ethicalwill.com)

Working Assets (www.workingassets.com). *Find an affinity credit card.*

Exchange, reuse, and recycling

AbeBooks (www.abebooks.com). *Search for secondhand books.*

Biketown USA (www.bicycling.com/biketown). *Send secondhand bikes to Africa.*

Book Crossing (www.bookcrossing.com). *Register books that you leave for others to read so that you can track them as they change hands.*

Direct Marketing Association (www.dmaconsumers.org). *Opt out of junk mail.*

Dump & Run™ (www.dumpandrun.org). *Student secondhand sales.*

Earth 911 (www.earth911.org)

Freecycle (www.freecycle.org). *Find a good home for unwanted items.*

The Health Equity Project (www.the healthequityproject.org). *Donate unused medicines.*

The Internet Consumer Recycling Guide (www.obviously.com/recycle/)

Title Trader (www.titletrader.com). *Swap books, DVDs, and CDs.*

Food and drink

Center for Food Safety (www.centerforfoodsafety.org)

Compassion in World Farming (www.ciwf.org)

The Ecological Farming Association (www.eco-farm.org)

Local Harvest (www.localharvest.org). *Find farmers' markets and Community Supported Agriculture programs in your area.*

Marine Stewardship Council (www.msc.org). *Search for sustainable seafood.*

Organic Consumers Association (www.organicconsumers.org)

Leisure

National Ski Areas Association (www.nsaa.org). *Includes a list of eco-friendly ski resorts.*

Organic Places to Stay (www.organicholidays.com)

Pioneer Thinking (www.pioneerthinking.com). *Craft techniques, including making paper.*

Reed Design (www.reeddesign.co.uk). *Make your own kite.*

Vegetarian Vacations (www.vegetarian-vacations.com)

Low-impact living

Eekos (www.eekos.com). *Information resource for sustainable living.*

Global Eco-village Network (www.ecovillage.org)

Green Building Resource Center (www.globalgreen.org/gbrc). *Search for green architects, builders, and building materials.*

Voluntary Simplicity (www.theworld.com/ ~ habib/thegarden//simplicity/)

Woodsmoke (www.woodsmoke.uk.com). *Camping techniques.*

Travel and transport

Better World Club (www.betterworldclub.com). *Car insurance with carbon offsets.*

Carbonfund.org (www.carbonfund.org). *Calculate and buy carbon offsets.*

CarSharing.net (www.carsharing.net). *Car clubs and car-share programs.*

Global Stewards (www.globalstewards.org/hotel.htm). *List of eco-tips for hotels.*

Green Hotels Association (www.greenhotels.com)

Institute for Transportation and Development Policy (www.itdp.org)

League of American Bicyclists (www.bikeleague.org)

Man in Seat 61 (www.seat61.com). *Plan flight-free journeys.*

The National Coalition of Walking Advocates (www.americawalks.org)

Travelers' Alert (www.bornfree.org.uk/travellers.alert). *Report animal cruelty while abroad.*

Water

Xeriscape (www.xeriscape.org). *Low-water gardening.*

INDEX

acne 175
aerosols 120–121
air conditioning 38–39, 180, 214, 246
 in cars 283
air fresheners 15, 75
alarm clocks 259
aluminum 137, 148, 258, 358–359
 foil 168, 255
angling 302
antifreeze 270, 302
ants 70–71
apes 154
arsenic 187
asphalt 113
auctions 166, 174
aviation 12, 72, 320
avocados 295

baby wipes 34
baking soda 15, 75, 159, 167, 255, 262
balloons 124
bamboo 59, 321, 362
banking, ethical 111
barbecues 118–119
baths and showers 85
batteries 29, 136, 248, 279
 chargers 136, 152
beach holidays 342
bedding 88
beekeeping 16
beer 224, 246–247
 beer bran 318
 homebrew 335
beeswax 62
bicycles 25, 81, 144
 couriers 237
 electric 143
 folding 143
 renting 299
 sharing 243
bio-diesel 316, 336
biodynamic wine 202–203
birds 290
 bird baths 338
 bird feeders 279
 bird houses 204
 birdwatching 158
 cat threat 80, 279
 pets 14–15
bleach 99, 151
Blue Wave beaches 342
boats 334, 367
bokashi composting 359
bonfires 164
books 91, 134, 201
borax 62, 123
Born Free Foundation 98
boron 113
brass, cleaning 168, 261–262
breastfeeding 35
bricks 166
building products 71
buildings, old 251
burial 124
butterflies 35, 194, 215

cameras 98
camping 58, 212–213, 293
 storm kettles 322
candles 28–29, 167
cans 132, 148–149, 358–359
carbon dioxide emissions 12, 17, 76, 218–219, 320, 323
 carbon footprint 17, 307
 Kyoto Protocol 218–219
 offsetting 12, 15, 111
carpets
 fastenings 171
 recycled 184
 restoration 237
cars
 air conditioning 283
 air filters 271
 antifreeze 270, 302
 batteries 279
 bio-diesel 316, 336
 catalytic converters 241
 clubs 78
 cruise control 91
 diesel fuel 316
 electric 248–250
 engine oil 149, 270–271, 304
 exhaust fumes 243–244
 flag-flying 287

fuel consumption 24, 91, 165, 179, 255, 316, 347
gas-electric hybrids 336
gears 271, 316
hydrogen-powered 141
insurance 269, 276
LPG (liquified petroleum gas) 336
luggage racks 178, 303
OBD (on-board diagnostic) system 274
off-road driving 244
pollution 149, 243–244, 304
recycling 358
servicing 273–274
sharing 60, 78, 142
tires 114, 139, 140–141, 165
traffic avoidance 276
trailers 303
washing 85–86
windshield-wiper fluid 302
catalytic converters 241
cats
cat litter 132
effect on wildlife 80, 279, 317
neutering 140
caviar 199
ceiling fans 182
cellars 162
cellphones 163, 329
chargers 104
cellulose 227, 239
chalk 62
charcoal 118–119
charities 68–69, 133, 163, 169, 196, 265, 280
chickens 159
children
baby food 34
baby wipes 34
bedding 88
breastfeeding 35
camping 293
clothes swapping 176
cycling 25, 81, 122–123, 140
diapers 33–34
farm visits 151
gardening 198, 340–341
green involvement 22, 40–41, 72, 151, 237
head lice 93
instilling a love of nature 103, 158, 173, 269, 293
organic food 289
party balloons 124
population growth 340
school journey 140
school uniform 212
toys 29, 32, 95, 100, 305, 356
chlorine 55, 99
chlorofluorocarbons (CFCs) 314
chocolate 347
Christmas
cards 68–69
decorations 188–189
lights 148
trees 253
chromated copper arsenate (CCA) wood preservative 187
chrome, cleaning 255
cigarettes 147, 366
circuses 289
cleaning 15
aluminum 258
brass 168, 261–262
chrome 255
cooktops 152
copper 261–262
detergents 55
disinfectants 52–53
drains 167
driveways and patios 176
glass 119
gold 219
microfiber cloths 324
mildew 282
ovens 255
paintbrushes 170
rust 68
shoes 261
silver 168
smells 168, 264
spilled drinks 43
stain removal 62, 347
stainless steel 258

teakettles 46
toilets 123
upholstery
windows 119, 283
climate change 17, 154, 191, 218–219, 257, 336
clocks, wind-up 259
clothing
artificial fibers 238, 239
children's 176
dry cleaning 62–63
dyes, natural 208
EcoSpun fiber 346
footwear 183, 196, 197
fur 182
hemp 109, 193
hot weather 52
jeans 50–51
knitting 260
organic cotton 50–51
recycling 133
school uniform 212
swapping 176, 326
vintage 162
coffee 239, 256–257
filters 228
machines 311
coffins 35
Community Supported Agriculture (CSA) 108–109
compact fluorescent lightbulbs (CFLs) 49, 103, 267
compost 112, 123, 164, 165, 166, 226, 244–245, 359
computers
Christmas greetings 68
energy-saving 46, 105
faxes 189
file storage 126
laptops 280
LCD screens 109, 310
paying bills online 55
power save mode 264, 299
printer cartridges 263
printers 263
recycling 121
shopping online 134, 362–363
shutdown 105, 235
voluntary work online 282–283
condoms 131
confetti 126
conservation projects 22–23, 114, 273
consumer action 24, 67, 94–95, 298–299
consumerism 315, 332
cookers 106
cooking 117, 272–273, 302
barbecues 118–119
cast-iron pans 200, 299
chopping boards 147, 362
energy-saving 23–24, 26, 44
mayonnaise 275
multi-meals 363
non-stick pans 200
oil disposal 247
one-pot 364
pressure cookers 26
solar ovens 344–345
soup from leftovers 328
steaming 272–273
stir-frying 58
stock 78
toaster ovens 180
vegetarian 137
copper
cleaning 261–262
recycling 290–291
coral 116, 218
cork 31
cosmetics 23, 56, 58, 75, 298, 303, 304, 338
cotton 50–51, 327
cream of tartar 258
credit cards 169
cremation 124
curtains 39
cycling 81, 122–123, 140, 142–143, 299, 332

decluttering 178
dehumidifiers, solar-powered 287
deodorants 159
diapers 33–34, 87, 88
diesel fuel 316

dishwashers 42–43, 103, 309
disinfectants 52–53
disposable products 67
DIY 52, 177
  BUDD rule 254
dogs 131, 291, 296
domestic equipment 70, 106, 276, 279, 309
  see also fridges and freezers
doormats 59
double glazing 39
drafts 78, 135, 160
drains 167
drapes 39
dry cleaning 62–63
ducks, feeding 178
Dump & Run™ sales 87
dyes, natural 208

E magazine 91
Earth Day 274
Earthwatch 227
eco-balls 88, 264
eco-exchange 353
EcoHomes standard (UK) 232
ecological footprints 157
Ecologist, The 91
eco-marathon 255
EcoSpun fiber 346–347
eco-villages 314–315
egg boxes 240
electricity
  lighting 48, 49, 99, 116, 323
  standby settings on appliances 50, 235, 251
  wiring 360
embalming 194
energy
  fridges and freezers 26–27, 46, 230
  geothermal 216
  hydroelectric power 113
  hydrogen fuel cells 141
  nuclear 351
  public use 311
  renewable 21, 76, 351
  saving 18, 23–24, 27, 32, 42–43, 48–49, 99, 103, 104, 105, 190, 230, 300, 302, 309, 320, 323, 333
  solar 300, 319
  tidal 333
  wind power 162–163
Energy Star 27, 275
energy-saving lightbulbs 116
engine oil 149, 270–271, 304
envelopes 145
essential oils 37, 175
ethics
  in business 318
  ethical banking 111
  ethical insurance 269
  ethical investing 326
  ethical pension funds 151
  tour operators 231
eucalyptus oil 262
European Eco-label 275
exhaust fans 105

fabric softener 253–254
face masks 307
Fairtrade 269, 287, 347
farmers' markets 330
faucets
  leaking 329
  low-flow fittings 98
faxes 189, 200
fish 195, 197, 205, 223, 230, 329
  fish farms 354–355
fish tanks 116
fishing 230
flame retardants 124
fleas 66
floor coverings 14, 259
  carpets 171, 184, 237
flowers, commercial 268–269
fly repellants 37
flying 12, 72, 320
food and drink
  baby foods 34
  beans 328
  beer 224
  caviar 199
  chocolate 347
  coffee 239, 256–257
  cost of production 164
  fast food 366–367
  fish 195, 197, 205, 223, 329, 354–355

fruit and vegetables 156, 222
GM foods 337, 360–361, 365
homemade 236
locally produced 90, 115, 231, 330
meat 30
milk 30–31, 364
nettles 215
organic 108, 289, 355
salads 108
seasonal 115
shrimp 222
Slow Food 30
soup from leftovers 328
takeout containers 112
tea 226, 228
tuna 44
turtles 358
vegetarian 30
wild 143
wine 38, 202–203, 209, 348
at work 88
"food miles" 90
footwear 183, 196, 197
polish 261
fossil fuels 17, 21
Freecycle movement 273, 353
fridges and freezers 26–27, 46, 51, 99, 133, 136, 230, 310, 323, 344, 350
frogs 119, 166, 248, 317
fruit and vegetables 156, 222
fungicides 268
fur 182
furniture 14
assembly 52
flame retardants 124
polish 62, 254
recycled 171, 184, 193
recycling 71

garage sales 178
garbage disposal units 266–267
gardening
bird baths 338
bird houses 204
bonfires 164
children's involvement 198, 340–341
cloches 164
community gardens 105
companion planting 47
compost 112, 207, 226, 359
crop rotation 104
fertilizers 207
ground cover 203
hanging baskets 116
hedges 214
lawns 12, 130, 205
leaf blowers 200
leaf mold 200, 250–251
micro-gardening 192
moles 284
mulching 42, 83
nettles 215
peat 112
pests and pesticides 47, 104, 112–113, 207
ponds 138–139, 166, 317
Popsicle stick plant labels 175
potatoes 114
rock gardens 119, 132
salads 108
slugs and snails 42, 43, 159
watering 12, 60, 82–83, 86, 168, 198, 207
weedkillers 210, 211
wild areas 22–23
wildflower meadows 146, 218
wildlife 35, 119, 126, 138–139, 166, 206, 214, 248, 290, 317
wormeries 215, 220
garlic 66
gas stoves 279
genetic modification
food labeling 337, 360–361, 365
GMOs (genetically modified organisms) 337, 365
geothermal heat pumps 216
gifts 41, 55, 94, 95, 139, 250, 265
wrapping 227

Ginkgo biloba 173
glaciers 257
glass 238
cleaning 119
recycling 110, 125, 129, 238, 357
Global Response 315
global warming 17, 37, 154, 218–219, 257
glycerin 62
gold, cleaning 219
golf, "green" 178–179
Gore, Al 257
Great Warming, The (TV show) 361
green building 71
green journals 53–54, 174
green mortgages 327
"greenfreeze" technology 133
greenhouse gases 12, 123, 218–219, 306–307
Grow-a-Note® paper 246
gyms 114, 162, 332

hair
dyes 296–297
hair care 93, 295
hairdryers 221
herbal treatments 266–267
rinsing 248
hand dryers 65
head lice 93
heating 18–19, 46, 49, 105, 139, 182, 217, 295
draft exclusion 78, 135, 160
duct leakages 224
furnace efficiency 18
geothermal heat pumps 216
insulation 19, 38, 39, 49, 162
patio heaters 47, 330
"tankless" water heaters 83
thermostats 50, 59
hedges 214
hemp
clothing 109, 193
paper 90
herbicides 22
herbs
eye treatments 129
hair treatments 266–267
insect repellants 167
moth repellants 28
tea 228
honey 16, 125, 307
HOURS program 294
house buying 232, 233
hydroelectric power 113
hydrogen power 141

Inconvenient Truth, An (movie) 257
insect repellants 37, 167, 198–199
insecticides 268
insulation 19, 38, 39, 162
insurance, ethical 269
interior decoration 51
International Buy Nothing Day 89–90
ironing 104, 120

jeans 50–51, 193
jewelry 163
junk mail 63, 243
jute 147

kettles 103
kitchen counter tops 175
kitchen fans 105
kitchen storage 232
kite-flying 180
knitting 260
Kyoto Protocol 218–219

latex 124, 131
paint 170
laundry 196–197, 211
diapers 33, 88
dry cleaning 62–63
eco-balls 88, 264
enzyme cleaning capsules 258
fabric softener 253–254
prewashes 338
steam washing machines 100
temperature 63
tumble dryers 92–93
washing machines 100, 276

washing powders 79, 233, 355
water saving 82
lavender 28, 66, 267
lawns 12, 205
lawnmowers 130
LCD (liquid crystal display) screens 109, 310
leaf blowers 200
leaf mold 200, 250–251
leather 183
LED (light-emitting diode) lights 148, 345, 357
LEED Green Building Rating System (USA) 232
lemonade 145
lemons
cleaning with 261, 262
moth deterrent 74
letter-writing campaigns 315, 352–353
lighting 48, 49, 99, 116, 323
outdoors 103
limescale 46
linoleum 259
Lions Club 51
litter 149, 190, 247
danger to wildlife 147, 246–247
lodgers 100
LPG (liquified petroleum gas) 336
lumber 120, 185

Macy, Joanna 22
mahogany 185
mail preference service 63
manuka honey 125
Marine Aquarium Council 116
Marine Stewardship Council 197
marker pens 346
mattresses 121
mayonnaise 275, 295
McDonough, William 77
meat production 30
medicines
natural 125, 175, 267
reuse 364
Medium Density Fiberboard (MDF) 120
menstrual cups 99
mentoring 321
mercury 267
methane 123
microfiber cleaning cloths 324
microwaves 300
mildew 282
milk, organic 30–31, 364
Millennium Ecosystem Assessment 23
mobiles 95
moles 284
Montreal Protocol 314
mortgages, green 327
moths 35, 210
deterrents 74
mothballs 28
movement sensors 48
MP3 players 94, 126
mulching 83
musk 75

nail polish 58
National Organic Program 304
nettles 215
newspapers 134
nuclear energy 351
nylon 238

oils
disposal 149, 247
engine oil 149, 270–271, 304
essential oils 37, 175
eucalyptus oil 262
lubricants 262
olive oil 261
palm oil 23
walnut oil 337
OLEDs (organic light-emitting diodes) 310
omega-3 fatty acids 31
organ donation 120
organic farms 116, 117, 151
organic products
baby formula 35
bedding 88

cosmetics and toiletries 304, 338
cotton 327
fish farms 355
food 108–109
milk 30–31, 364
wine 348
wool 106
owls 126
oysters 173
ozone 55, 314

packaging 66–67, 70
paints 18, 54, 56, 170–171
paintbrushes 170
stripper 186
thinnner 253
palm oil 23
paper
giftwrap 95
Grow-a-Note® 246
hemp 90
logs 134
making paper 325
recycled 91, 95, 126, 131, 147, 151
recycling 15, 74, 128, 353
saving 228, 234, 238
tissues 184
use 68, 71
parabens 56, 338
parchment paper 191
pashmina wool 111
patio heaters 47, 330
PBDE flame retardant 124
Peace Corps 282
peat 112
pencils 202
pens 128, 202
pension funds 151
perfumes 75, 298
pesticides 22, 112–113, 176, 327, 363
pets
birds 14–15
cat litter 132
dog poop 131
exotic 136
fish 116
fleas 66
food 132, 195, 296
neutering 140
rescued 119
wildlife threat 80
phenology 336
phone directories 238
phosphate pollution 233
photovoltaic panels 300
plants 302
for butterflies and moths 35
companion planting 47
drought-tolerant 82, 119
gifts 250
insect repellants 167
moth repellants 28
pest-resistant varieties 47
pollution absorption 20
plastic 33, 238
bags 144–145
in computers 121
litter 246–247
PVC 29, 186, 259, 360
reuse 129, 164, 175, 209
recycling 33, 129, 348
toys 29
plates, disposable 263
polar bears 154
police auctions 166
polishes 62
pollution
car exhaust 40, 243–244
hazardous waste 97, 112–113
in the home and office 20
oceans 157
reporting 12
water 112–113, 213, 233, 247, 304
polyester 238
polystyrene 266
ponds 138–139, 166
popcorn 158
Popsicle sticks 175
population growth 340
potatoes 114
power tools 54
preservatives 113, 187
pressure cookers 26
printers 68, 263
cartridges 263
PVC 29, 186, 259, 360

radiators 18–19
rain forests 152
rainwater 308
rayon 239
razors 160, 286
recycling 59, 234, 277, 291, 294, 357
aluminum 137, 148–149
batteries 279
bicycles 144
carpets 184
cars 358
cellphones 163
Christmas cards 69
Christmas trees 253
clothing 133
computers 121
copper 290–291
engine oil 149
eyeglasses 51
footwear 196
Freecycle 273, 353
fridges and freezers 136
furniture 71
glass bottles 110, 125, 129, 238, 357
newspaper 15, 134
packaging 70
paper 74, 128, 353
plastics 33, 129, 348
polystyrene 266
school use 72
sorting 294
swapping and selling 101
tires 140–141
vinyl 190
rosemary 28, 66, 267
rosewater 306
rosewood 298
rubber bands 286
rum 363
running 291, 332–333
rust removal 68

sailing 367
salt, cleaning with 43, 168, 262
sanitary products 99
schools
buses 40
eco-marathon 255
green involvement 29, 41, 140, 269
nature trips 100
recycling 72
travel to 140
uniform 212
SERVAS organization 37
shading a house 343
sharpening stones 187
shatoosh wool 111
shaving 12, 159–160, 286
shoe polish 261
shopping 41
avoiding 37, 89
books 91, 134
consumer power 24, 67, 94–95, 298–299
domestic equipment 26, 70, 100, 180, 309
Fairtrade 269, 287, 347
food 41
lists 295
local shops 350, 365
online 134, 362–363
organic 176–177
packaging 66–67
product labeling 56, 274–275, 357
sales 128
shrimp 222
silver, cleaning 168
skiing 133, 216
skill sharing 261
skin care 306, 307
Slow Food 30
slugs and snails 42, 43
smoke detectors 302–303
smoking 147, 366
soda water 347
Soil Association (UK) 304
solar energy 21, 76, 142, 300
backpacks 319
battery chargers 94, 136
dehumidifiers 287
mole deterrents 284
panels 319
solar ovens 344–345
water heating 50
Soweto Mountain of Hope (Somoho) 60

sports, environmental impact 230–231
stain removal 62, 347
standby settings 251
staples 64
stargazing 58
steam washing machines 100
steel 318
  stainless 258–259
stilt-walking 143
stir-fry cooking 58
storm kettles 322
streetlights 311
sugar cane 363
sunbeds 309
sunscreen 288–289
swimming pools 278–279
swordfish 329

teak 185
teeth, brushing 79
television 187, 209, 296
  LCD screens 109
  sleep timer 258
  standby settings 235, 251
Tencel® fiber 239
Thermos® flasks 103
thyme 267
tidal energy 333
tires 114, 139, 140–141, 165
toaster ovens 180
toasters 244
tobacco 22
toiletries 303, 304, 338
toilets
  cleaning 123
  flushing 86–87, 144
  heated seats 332
  leaks 199
toys 95, 100, 305, 356
traffic signals 357
trains 81
travel 81, 177, 231, 334
  avoiding 128
  carbon offsetting 12, 111
  flying 12, 72
  insurance 269
trees 185
  planting 65, 366
tumble dryers 92–93
tuna 44
turpentine 31
turtles 358

UN online volunteering program 282–283
USB flash drives 126
utility bills 53–54

vacations 72, 116, 117, 133, 137, 216, 226–227, 231, 242–243, 299, 320
  camping 212–213
vanilla essence 58
vending machines 41, 328–329
video conferencing 128
vinegar 46, 62, 68, 119, 123, 167, 219, 248, 254, 255, 259, 262, 264, 282, 283, 302, 347
vinyl 190
viscose 239
volatile organic compounds (VOCs) 31, 54, 171, 186
voluntary work 235, 261, 273, 282
voting 136–137

walking 95, 142–143, 280, 332–333
  stilts 143
wallpaper 147, 186
walnut oil 337
washing see laundry
washing dishes 79, 103, 209
washing machines 100, 276
waste
  into art 60
  compostable matter 123
  garage sales 178
  hazardous 97, 112–113
  in manufacturing 77
  oceans and seas 157
  reuse 241
  swapping 101
  toxic metals 136
water
  bottled 74–75
  "gray" water use 83

habitats 273
heating 83, 295
hydroelectric power 113
leaks 93, 171, 199, 329
meat production 30
rainwater gathering 308
saving 14, 74–75, 79, 85–87, 98, 117, 144, 190, 276, 286
swimming pools 278–279
tidal power 333
watering the garden 60, 82–83, 86, 168
waterbeds 262
water sports 220
wave power 21
wax polish 254
weatherstripping 160
weddings
confetti 126
lists 124
travel to 111
weedkillers 210, 211
weevils 167
wild flowers 146, 218, 246
wildlife 154, 259, 290, 291
animal cruelty 98
birdwatching 158
butterflies and moths 194, 210
cat threat 80
conservation 229
feeding 286
in the garden 119, 126, 138–139, 146, 166, 206, 248
litter hazard 246–247
products 90
turtles 358
urban 284–285
wills, making 125
wind power 21, 76, 162–163
windows
cleaning 283
draperies 194
windshield-wiper fluid 302
wind-up mechanism 142
wine 38, 202–203, 209, 348
wood 120
as habitat 206
chopping boards 147
fuel 242
for furniture 14
preservatives 113, 187
pulp 239
waste 165
wool 106, 111, 116
workplace
car sharing 142
clothing 52
compost production 244–245
energy saving 324
environmental officers 352
food and drink 23, 88, 113, 126, 131
green involvement 29, 64, 324
marker pens 346
paper saving 68, 131, 234
pens and pencils 128, 202
recycling 128, 173, 353
time off for voluntary work 235
vending machines 328–329
Worldwatch Institute 312
World-Wide Opportunities on Organic Farms (WWOOF) 116
wormeries 215, 220

yoga mats 292
yogurt 307

ACKNOWLEDGMENTS

Page 315: quotation from *Eco-Economy* by Lester R. Brown. Copyright © 2001 by Earth Policy Institute. Used by permission of W.W. Norton & Company, Inc.